Don’t Tell The Bride

THE ALTERNATIVE GUIDE TO THE ULTIMATE WEDDING

Don't Tell The Bride...

Published by Blink Publishing
107-109 The Plaza, 535 King's Road, Chelsea Harbour, London, SW10 0SZ

www.blinkpublishing.co.uk
facebook.com/blinkpublishing
twitter.com/blinkpublishing

978 1 91053 626 1

A CIP catalogue of this book is available from the British Library.

Design by Steve Leard
leard.co.uk

Printed and bound by Interak, Poland

1 3 5 7 9 10 8 6 4 2

Papers used by Blink Publishing are natural, recyclable products made from wood grown in sustainable forests. The manufacturing processes conform to the environmental regulations of the country of origin.

Blink Publishing is an imprint of the Bonnier Publishing Group
www.bonnierpublishing.co.uk

Don't Tell the Bride is produced by Renegade Pictures Limited which is part of the Shed Media Group Limited

Acknowledgements

Renegade Pictures UK would like to thank all the couples that so kindly shared their wedding experiences for this book, as well as every bride and groom who have appeared in *Don't Tell The Bride* throughout the years, along with their friends and families, to make it such a TV treat. We'd also like to thank all the venues and bridal suppliers who have provided services for our couples, and Matt Whyman, Jordan Paramor, Blink Publishing and Lucas Alexander Whitley for making this book happen.

Introduction

It's 11.30 at night. I'm slumped in front of the TV watching a repeat of something I didn't enjoy the first time round. Meanwhile my fiancée is frantically scanning through websites desperate to find a venue for our impending wedding. When the adverts come on I think I notice a look of something between panic and frustration on her face. Even to an insensitive soul like me, it's clear that trying to organise '*our big day*' is turning into a nightmare. All the posh venues have been booked years ago, half the family can't do the dates we want to do and the dress… well, she hasn't had time to think about the dress.

Naturally, I haven't even thought about the dress, or the guests or the venue, or indeed anything to do with the nuptials. Blokes just turn up at weddings in a hired suit, do what they're told and then drink as much as they can, right? Unlike a bride-to-be, we haven't been keeping scrapbooks since we were little or spent any time fantasising about our big day – it's just not in our DNA. But it was obvious, even to me, that trying to put together the happiest day of your life can make you miserable.

That was when I had a very stupid idea. 'I'll do it!' I thought. 'I'll sort out the wedding. How difficult can it be?'

In short, it was the toughest thing I have ever done – more painful than having my appendix removed and more frustrating than watching England at a World Cup. But despite all the aggravation, and after a few man-tears, we finally found ourselves, three weeks later, standing in a 19th-century chapel at the end of the Las Vegas strip. A preacher, who looked more like a magician's assistant, conducted the ceremony and our families watched the whole thing bleary-eyed on webcams back in the UK.

Not only did it prove to be a bizarre but brilliant couple of days, it was the inspiration for the TV show *Don't Tell The Bride* and the book you're about to read. As for the lesson from that special day and the hundreds of weddings that followed, it's really very simple. If you let the man in your life organise your wedding then you won't necessarily get the day that you wanted... but it will be one you'll never forget.

Jon Rowlands – a bloke who tried to organise a wedding and ended up with a TV show.

Chris & Corrine

The Dream Day

Everyone wants his or her wedding to be memorable. What matters is that people look back on the big day for all the right reasons. So, what goes into turning the dream into a reality? Is there a role for taking risks or pushing boundaries, and how do couples cope when things don't go to plan?

For most brides-in-waiting and grooms-to-be, it's a question of working as a team. Whether it's a low-key event or a grand extravaganza, the event requires strategic thinking and the ability to work under pressure just to make it happen. To turn it into a special occasion is another matter entirely, and demands a big heart as much as a level head. It makes sharing the load a smart move, as most couples will agree. But what happens when just one half shoulders the responsibility – and potentially the blame?

Chris and Corrine – The fairy tale wedding

'To turn it into a special occasion is another matter entirely, and demands a big heart as much as a level head.'

By his own admission, Chris is a big kid at heart with wild ideas. 'There's "a little bit crazy"', says his other half, Corrine, three years his junior and definitely the grown up in the relationship, 'and then there's "Chris crazy".'

Born and raised in a sleepy Scottish village, nightclub DJ Chris moved to Doncaster where he met his future wife. It wasn't love at first sight for Corrine, a level-headed and homely type, though ultimately what won her over was Chris's sheer lust for life. 'I am the exuberant eccentric,' says the man with a passion for Mad-Hatter headwear, wild declarations and an

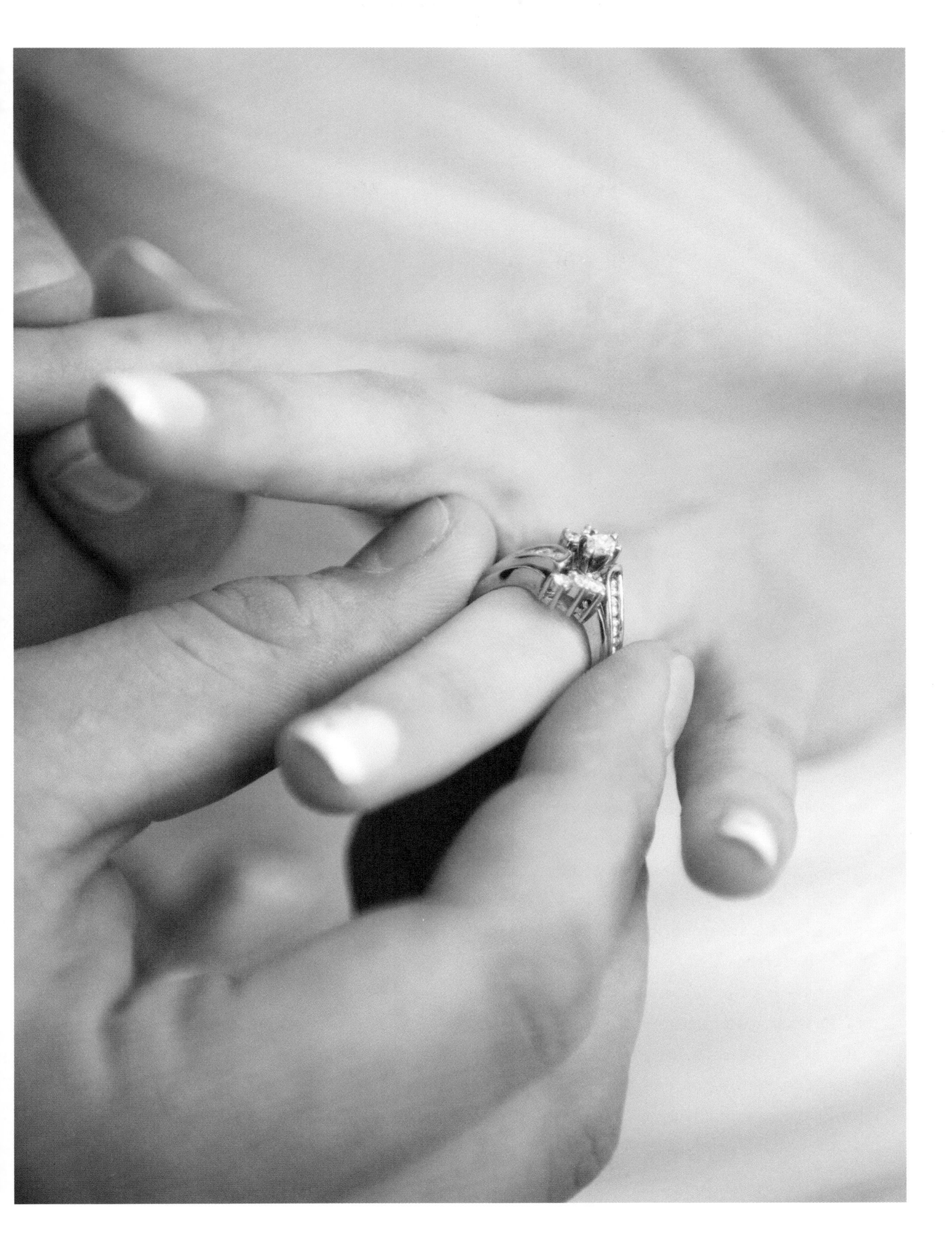

impressively waxed moustache, 'and Corrine is the anchor that grounds me.'

With a son they both adore, and another one on the way, Chris decided to pop the question – and Corrine responded with an overwhelming 'yes!'

As new parents, she says, 'it seemed like the most natural thing to do. For me, the strongest point in our relationship is that Chris is such a brilliant dad. He would spend all his time with our son Oscar, and we wanted to build on that.'

As Chris saw things, fatherhood was the trigger that made him look at life in a different way. 'All the soppy, sentimental stuff that never meant much to me suddenly transformed in my mind. I didn't just want Corrine to be my wife. Nor did I simply want to give her the wedding day she deserved. It had to be something she enjoyed. After all, I absolutely adore the woman,' he explains, 'so why would I want to put her in a position, on the most important day of her life, where she feels awkward or is left questioning my decisions?'

In making Corrine's dreams come true, Chris decided there could only be one way forward – and that involved turning a fairy tale into reality. 'It's the word that everyone uses to describe the perfect wedding,' he explains. 'I wanted to get back to the true meaning and create a special day for my bride that actually felt like it had come from a childhood storybook. In my mind, that was the definition of a dream day.'

> **'You want the day to be just perfect, of course, but however you choose to stage it, what matters most is your commitment to each other.'**

So, you want to get married?

In many ways, popping the question is guaranteed to leave couples with their heads in the clouds. And why not? It's a big deal, whichever way you slice the cake. We're talking about an expression of everlasting love between two people and a commitment to spending the rest of their lives together. It's no wonder that many get carried away at this moment, and aim high when it comes to their plans for the big day.

There's nothing wrong with having an ambitious outlook, of course, but Chris warns that it needs be grounded with a serious reality check. 'I had ridiculously grandiose ideas like getting married on a steampunk pirate ship. It was epic in my mind, but doomed from the start, and yet that kind of blue-sky thinking is important in the evolution of your dream day. It helps you to work out the boundaries between what's realistic and what's sheer fantasy. Money played a big factor here, but what truly scuppered my dream of a wedding on the high seas was the fact that Corrine would've been required to wear a life jacket over her bridal gown. Frankly, it was out of the question, and that's when I started to focus and refine my ideas.'

Of course, it's natural to feel disappointed on accepting that your vision of getting married in space isn't going to happen (without a billion-pound budget). As well as grounding your ambitions in the realms of the possible, something else can come from scrapping such ideas, and that's the focus it brings on the reasons why you're getting married in the first place. You want the day to be just perfect, of course, but however you choose to stage it, what matters most is your commitment to each other.

'People kept saying I looked so calm,' says Corrine, looking back on her wedding day. 'But even when the bridesmaids suggested that things were threatening to go wrong, I never lost faith in Chris. There's always method in his madness, and I knew that he'd throw himself into the task. In the end, what he achieved was amazing,' she adds. And having been apart for three weeks, exactly how did she feel? 'It was better than anything I could've imagined, but by then I could've been driven to a ceremony in a rain-swept car park and I wouldn't have been disappointed. At the end of the day, if Chris had put his heart and soul into it, and we ended up married, nothing else mattered to me.'

Be creative

Money is certainly a big factor when it comes to working out how to make your wedding dreams come true. Budgeting is central here, but it doesn't have to dictate the vision. If anything, as Chris discovered, it can force you to be inventive. 'Once I'd decided on a woodland fairy tale theme, I realised there was still a lot of stuff I couldn't afford. For example, I wanted Corrine to enter the woodland through a *Narnia*-inspired wardrobe. I looked at hiring a theatre prop, but that was going to set me back £800. So, instead, I just bought one for £40 and kicked the back out of it. Dressed up with drapes it looked amazing, and provided just the entrance I could've hoped for at a fraction of the price. Being flexible is what saved the day for me. Had I stuck to my guns, the money would've disappeared in a second, and I'm proud of the fact that I didn't just abandon my plans and play it safe. I think if all couples did that it would make life just a little less exciting.'

Be cool

'From a catering catastrophe to dress disasters, anything that could go wrong may well go very wrong indeed... what matters is how you handle it.'

Even if your dream wedding day goes without a hitch, the chances are the planning stages will feature surprises and even the odd nightmare. From a catering catastrophe to dress disasters, anything that could go wrong may well go very wrong indeed. With so much at stake, it's only to be expected. What matters is how you handle it.

Whether you set out as a couple to make your dream day come true, or you've taken on that role alone, make sure you seek support from the people who know you best of all. We're talking about those who share your desire to make it happen and can help to lighten the load: your closest friends and family.

'I genuinely wouldn't have been able to get through the three weeks in the run-up to the wedding if it wasn't for the team of guys I assembled around me,' says Chris. 'My best man and best friends just bent over backwards to help, and often went beyond the call of duty. In the absence of Corrine, I even had one of them model a wedding dress for me! In the run up to the big day I had an uncle cutting up straw bales so people could sit on them, and other family members painting giant toadstools. They saw I had this great burden of responsibility, and did whatever was needed to help me out. Everyone just pulled together, simply so I could deliver my vision.'

As well as providing manpower, your friends and family provide another vital role: emotional support. At a time when stress levels often run high, every wedding plan is likely to get damp with tears at some stage or another. 'I was eight months pregnant and hormonal,' laughs Corrine. 'My bridesmaids genuinely made everything so much easier. Even if I just wanted to let off steam they would listen, and that quickly helped me to get things into perspective.'

For Chris, who had undertaken to marry his bride in a remote woodland glade, having a shoulder to cry on was essential in keeping the plan on track. 'There were times when I felt so low and exhausted both physically and mentally, and this reached a peak on the night before the wedding. I'd spent all the money, and was sharing a room with my best man and two friends. We were knackered, having driven all day, and I felt absolutely wretched. I couldn't sleep as I was about to get married, but they got me through. It helped to remind me that I was about to see Corrine the next day, and share this dream I'd worked so hard to make happen.'

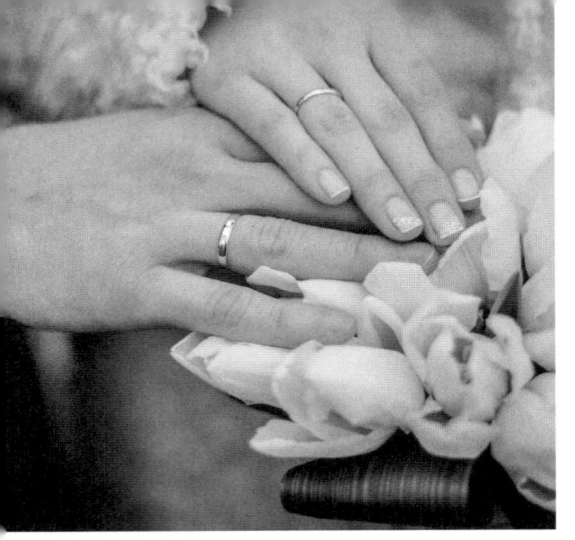

A dream come true

'I was there to marry the woman I loved. What more could I have asked for?'

After all the blood, sweat and tears that go into creating a wedding, the day itself can seem unreal. Finally, after all the effort that you've put into making your dream event come true, having overcome setbacks and unleashed your creative spirit, it all plays out for real – and you're in the hands of fate.

So how does it feel when that moment arrives? Does the reality measure up the dream, or can it ever compare? 'My aim from the start was that in years to come people would tell the story of our wedding,' says Chris, 'as if it had become a fairy tale in itself. I hope I pulled that off, but everything changed the moment I finally laid eyes on Corrine. I just felt like a giddy teenager, and that put the whole day into perspective for me. I was there to marry the woman I loved. What more could I have asked for?'

For Corrine, the effort Chris had made was apparent as soon as she stepped out of the wedding car. 'It wasn't what I expected, but I loved it. Every detail was down to him, and that literally made my day. Even the sun decided to come out from behind the rain clouds, but it could've poured and it wouldn't have changed anything. It was truly magical, which is just what he intended.'

Looking back at a wedding the couple consider to be a dream come true, what advice do Chris and

Corrine have for couples planning their big day? 'It all boils down to having faith in each other,' says Corrine. 'With so much to consider, and things to get done, there can be times when it feels overwhelming. You need to be able to trust the person you're marrying with your heart and soul. Even if you're physically apart at the time, if you know you're in this together then really nothing can go wrong. At the end of the day, no matter what happens, you'll always be there for each other.' In Chris's view, there's just one essential factor in making your day just perfect. 'Everything else is down to you as a couple and what you'd like to include,' he begins, 'but the one thing you both have to carry with you is the simple desire to get married. It doesn't matter if it rains, or your bride rips her dress, or your dad ruins the photo because he's a bit drunk. The sole reason you're there, in front of everyone, is to say "I do" to each other.'

Highlights from the Show...
The Dream Day

David and Lucy – Pride and Prejudice

What better way to woo his bookish bride than by staging a wedding based on Jane Austen's classic novel? David knows he's onto a winner, despite never having read the book. Cue three weeks in which our groom seriously wings it, but pulls things together with a mixture of charm, luck and sheer determination. Finally, the big day beckons and Lucy is transported back to an age of Regency romance and Darcy-like dazzle. 'I've got nothing bad to say,' she declares, admiring her groom's hard work. 'It looks amazing!'

Josh and Stacie – the Jam-Irish wedding of the year

'In general,' says Josh bravely, 'Stacie pretty much gets what she wants.' So, when it comes to their wedding, and Stacie's dream of a traditional church affair, Josh throws caution to the wind by laying on a wedding that celebrates their Irish and Jamaican roots. Following a trip to the party shop, to try out a leprechaun outfit and dreadlock wig, the groom and his best man realise they need to up their game considerably to avoid causing offence. Josh does this in style – devoting time and effort to creating the perfect reception for his bride. 'Amazing!' smiles Stacie, blissfully unaware of what prompted this upswing in effort.

Alex and Kara – Going conventional

Do all brides dream of a traditional white wedding? Not Kara, whose idea of a perfect ceremony would be one that takes place in a cave. If only she'd told groom Alex, who instead goes into conservative overdrive with a summer fête theme. Every effort he makes seems doomed to fall flat for his unconventional fiancée. Then Kara steps into the walled garden that hosts his big surprise, and turns expectations upside down by shedding nothing but happy tears. 'I wouldn't have thought of doing this,' she beams later. 'But I love it!'

Cameron and Sarah – In the clouds

Cameron is desperate to impress his bride-to-be, but he also wants to arrange a wedding that he thinks his parents will love. Pleasing everyone will be tough, but Sarah is hoping he'll at least put her first. And pleasing his bride isn't Cameron's only worry, because Sarah's sister is also getting married. What's more, it's the kind of traditional wedding that Sarah would love to have for herself. In a fix like this, Cameron is forced to aim high – and hires a helicopter to fly her to the ceremony. 'This could not have been further from what I wanted,' says Sarah once her feet are on the ground once more. 'But it's just been perfect.'

Adam and Lydia – Lookalike love

Big spender Adam aims to bling up his wedding to Lydia. His ambition? To create an A-List event, attended by celebrities such as Simon Cowell and Britney Spears… or at least their professional lookalikes. As the wedding car pulls up in front of the red carpet, the bride in the backseat spots two familiar figures and her jaw drops. 'It's not actually, is it?' she asks. 'Is it actually?' Well, no, it isn't, but even that doesn't deter Lydia from having the time of her life.

Darren & Bronte

Blowing the Budget

In an ideal world we'd have a never-ending pot of cash to make our big day as showstopping as possible. But unless you're Kim Kardashian or Kanye West there are going to have to be compromises.

Whether it's replacing your dream designer dress with something off the peg or booking an Ed Sheeran tribute act instead of the real thing (which would set you back an eye-watering £75,000), there are plenty of ways to get married in fabulous fashion within your budget.

Bronte and Darren – The hap-brie couple

'There are plenty of ways to get married in fabulous fashion within your budget...'

When Cambridge natives Darren and Bronte first met, it wasn't exactly a match made in heaven. But when they caught each other's eyes over a cheese sandwich at a party, Bronte had a feeling she could be onto something gouda. 'I was friends with Darren's sister at school and one night she had a party and Darren was there with his mates. They were all acting like total idiots and I wasn't impressed. I was actually dating Darren's ex-girlfriend's ex-boyfriend at the time. I'd heard some bad things about him, so that didn't help either. Then Darren randomly made me a cheese sandwich that night and we had a chat, and I really warmed to him. When I split up with the other guy, Darren asked me out and I decided I had nothing to lose!'

The pair soon fell for each other, but as Darren was due to move to Switzerland the following week their romance looked doomed. As Bronte says: 'We went for a walk at Wimpole Hall in Cambridge for our first date. It was just before my 18th birthday and a week before Darren was leaving

to go to Switzerland for work. We hung out every day that week and the day after my 18th he went away for six months. My mum and I drove him to Dover, and I cried my eyes out when he left. We'd only been seeing each other a week but I was devastated. We spoke every day on Skype and I went to visit him a month later. A week after I left, Darren moved back to England and I was so happy. We were inseparable after that.'

Darren proposed three years later on Bronte's 21st birthday at the very same place they had their first date. 'We went for a walk at Wimpole Hall, which is obviously a place we both love,' recalls Darren. 'Bronte had suggested that I invite some friends along with us but I managed to dissuade her so it was just the two of us. I had the ring in my pocket and I had to keep moving it around because I was so worried about losing it. I got down on one knee and when Bronte realised what was going on she swore, cried and then eventually said "yes". She phoned her mum straight away and I think because we were quite young the first thing she said to her was "are you sure?" Thankfully she didn't change her mind, though. I organised a dinner for her and all of her friends that night, so it was a double birthday and engagement celebration.'

In need of some Alp

The couple both made the decision to apply for *Don't Tell The Bride*. When they were accepted, Darren knew just how to make his and Bronte's wedding day incredible. 'I'd always liked the idea of getting married

in Switzerland. When I lived there I found out you could get married in a grotto on the top of the Alps and I loved the idea of us skiing down the mountain afterwards. It was pretty stressful organising it all. The first couple of days seemed to go really well, but the more in-depth the planning got, the less confident I became that I could organise everything on time. I don't think it helped that I went out partying the day before I was due to look at reception venues!'

Thankfully he had a lot of support in the shape of his best men, twins Ben and Dan. 'They helped me sort out loads of stuff and I was so grateful. I think there's always a danger of feeling like a butler at your own wedding because you're running around so much, so it's really nice to have people who can help to take some of the pressure off. We had two-way radios and stayed in touch at all times, so I was always in the loop, but I managed to relax and have fun too.'

As she'd never skied before, Bronte was initially horrified when a pair of ski boots arrived at her door on the day of the wedding. But once her panic subsided she decided to embrace every moment. 'I thought Darren might send me winter boots to wear because of the snow but I really wasn't expecting ski boots. Obviously I realised straight away that we would be skiing at some point, but I had no idea what else Darren had planned. It was all a massive surprise to me and I loved it all.'

How chalet cut costs?

Today, the average cost of a wedding is £20,000, and it's incredibly easy for costs to spiral out of control when you're in the thick of organising everything, so buy a notebook or start a spreadsheet, and note down each and every thing you book or buy (no matter how small). This way you can keep a very close eye on how much you have left to spend, and it will help to keep you on the straight and narrow. Ask yourself:

- **Is anyone (friends and family) helping you with costs?**
- **Would it be financially viable to take out a loan/get a credit card?**
- **How much money are you realistically able to save up as a couple between now and your nuptials?**

Here are some other handy ways to save money:

- **Get married mid-week or out of season (i.e. autumn or winter).**
- **Ask a friend to do the photography/ videography for you as your wedding present.**
- **Hire outfits instead of buying them.**
- **Make your own invites, place cards and thank you cards.**
- **Make your own favours.**
- **Be discerning with your guest list.**
- **Have a pay bar.**
- **Make your own playlists so you don't have to splash out on a DJ.**

If you want to be clever with your cash, as well as buying things on Ebay where they're often a fraction of the price they are in shops, consider selling on the website too. Most people have things lying around their house they no longer need, and it takes no time to list items. Alternatively you could sell things through local papers and even on Facebook.

Also consider that you may be able to scrape back some money after the event. If you're happy to sell your dress rather than store it in the attic for the next 50 years there's a huge market for second-hand wedding gowns.

If you're having unusual centrepieces and don't know what to do with them afterwards, flog them as a job lot. In short, if you can resist the strong temptation to get emotionally attached to your wedding goods there's some serious money to be made.

Switzerland is one of the world's most expensive countries, so how on earth did Darren manage to stay within his £12,000 budget? With some very, very careful planning and a willingness to compromise. 'When you watch people on *Don't Tell The Bride* trying to organise a wedding in the UK on that budget it's hard enough, but I had to try and get 50 people to Switzerland. It was always going to be a challenge but we cut costs wherever we could and I had to keep the purse strings as tight as possible. We stayed in the cheapest hostel we could find, which was above a nightclub so it wasn't exactly quiet. We also searched around for the cheapest flights. They turned out to be from Gatwick, and even though it wasn't hugely convenient we did save a lot because they weren't at off-peak times. It meant we had to get a taxi home to Cambridge at 2am the day after the wedding and I had to be up for work at 7am, but the bottom line was that I had to compromise.'

Darren advises people to watch out for hidden costs when booking and buying – and negotiate hard. 'Some of the things I thought would be expensive turned out to be quite reasonable, and vice versa. For instance, I thought a lot of the budget would have to go on Bronte's hotel but I negotiated as much as possible. One of the chalets Bronte stayed in should have been £1,000 per night per chalet, but I managed to get two for two nights for the same money. My job as a procurement manager means I have to negotiate things on a daily basis so that came in very handy and I got some great savings. One thing I will say is try and get as many things from the same place as possible so you can try and get a deal. The more you buy the more bargaining power you have. I found that people were more willing to work with me if I was spending a lot of money so it becomes more collaborative. Don't be afraid to be cheeky.'

Bootiful savings

'The biggest piece of advice I can give is that you can do things yourself. You don't have to spend hundreds.'

Even though the couple's festive-themed wedding looked amazing, Darren found even more cunning ways to be frugal, including scouring a sale rail for the bridesmaids' dresses. 'When we went to the wedding dress shop I was a bit clueless. My maximum budget was £1,000 but the one I really wanted was £1,700. In the end the shop owner felt a bit sorry for me so she knocked off £500 and threw in all of the tailoring. I also got a bargain with the bridesmaids' dresses because the owner had some she was trying to get rid of that were on the sale rail so she did me an amazing deal. I saved a small fortune on the shoes as well because Bronte wore ski boots so I didn't need to buy any. She ended up wearing trainers from Primark when she later took the boots off. And I didn't have to book expensive transport because we got an electro car that was owned by the chalet. My sister Sally is a make-up artist and Bronte did her own hair so I saved money there too.'

Bronte thinks Darren did an amazing job with the money he had, but there were a few things that had to be sacrificed so he didn't overspend. 'If I'd had my dream wedding I would have wanted my nieces and nephews as part of the wedding party but the budget didn't stretch to Darren flying them over and buying them

'If you know anyone who is going on holiday or you have friends and family who live abroad you could always ask them to see if they can pick up designer rings more cheaply.'

outfits so that wasn't possible. But he did brilliantly overall. The biggest piece of advice I can give is that you can do things yourself. You don't have to spend hundreds. The cake was homemade and it would have cost Darren a fortune to buy a proper one but it did the job.'

Ring the Changes

Rings can eat up a hefty amount of your budget so you want to get yourself the best deal possible. You'll have them for the rest of your lives so most importantly make sure you get something you like!

If you don't mind having something plain and simple you can pick up bands in any high street jewellers. If you want something a bit more special head to London's famous jewellery corner, Hatton Garden, or Birmingham's jewellery quarter, which produces an estimated 40 percent of all the UK's jewellery. You can also scour jewellery markets and second-hand shops around the country. Not only will you find something more unusual, but you're more likely to be able to haggle and get the price down.

You'll be able to get your hands on a 9-carat gold ring for around £100–£150, but as soon as you move on to a higher carat gold or platinum the price starts to rise. If you know anyone who is going on holiday or you have friends and family who live abroad you could always ask them to see if they can pick up designer rings more cheaply.

'Every time I look at our photos I'm reminded of how special it all was...'

Often jewellery bought in America will work out far more reasonable than it does in the UK depending on the exchange rate. So if you're splashing out a hefty amount it's definitely worth checking.

Hap-ski ever after

Darren and Bronte are now living happily in a small village outside Cambridge with their cocker spaniel, Milo. As well as working full time, Darren is running a company, with his business partner Ben, called Cambridge Garden Care, while Bronte is a charity worker for Addenbrooke's Hospital. Two years on, Bronte is still basking in the glow of her incredible day. 'We've got a mid-Georgian terrace which is absolutely beautiful and we're really happy with our naughty dog. I'll always have amazing memories of my wedding day and I feel so lucky we got such a brilliant opportunity. Every time I look at our photos I'm reminded of how special it all was.'

Highlights from the Show… Blowing the Budget

Jack and James – The cake table on a shoestring

Jack plans to save some pennies when it comes to organising his wedding to James. Together with his best man, he cooks up a plan to make a cake table using only the finest raw materials – namely a stack of pallets in the yard outside their house. Firstly, however, the deep-cover duo needs to sneak back and extract the pallets without being spotted. James may be away, but that doesn't guarantee the house is unoccupied. So, can Jack succeed in pulling off this daring, *Mission Impossible*-style operation without being busted? In short, no.

Jess and Luke – Mutiny of the bridesmaids

Luke is well aware that he needs to cover the cost of the bridesmaids' dresses. The trouble is there are just so many of them! And whose fault is that, he reminds his best mates? Yeah. Exactly. So, Luke hatches a money-saving plan, which involves standing awkwardly in front of the girls in the shop and gently breaking the news that they'll each need to stump up £80 for the privilege of wearing the outfits of his choice. The bridesmaids gather for a whispered meeting behind closed curtains, before returning with an ultimatum: cough up the cash or there won't be any bridesmaids. Luke responds constructively by walking out of the shop.

Daina and Ahmet – What price sexy?

Ahmet arrives to show the two bridesmaids the dresses he's selected for them. Stepping inside, he might as well be carrying a pair of handkerchiefs. Still, at £11 a dress it's a material saving in more ways than one. Gamely, the girls agree to squeeze into his outfits of choice. Ahmet waits patiently for their reappearance. Then the door opens up and the groom's eyes pop out on stalks. 'That's niiiice,' he tells them, checking out their figure-hugging red halter-necks. 'Yeah,' comes the reply. 'For *clubbing*!'

Paul and Emily – Go figure

Enter Paul – so financially challenged he receives pocket money from his fiancée. 'She gives me £1.50 a day,' he grumbles. 'It's like being at school.' So, when presented with the opportunity to spent £12,000 on a dream day, our groom reacts like a kid in a sweetshop. Burning through the cash, Paul even resorts to plundering the couple's personal bank account to keep himself afloat. 'I'm going to kill him,' mutters Emily on checking the balance. Luckily for Paul, she ditches the death threat for a soppy kiss on seeing the effort he's made to fund her perfect day.

Anna and Sian – Priceless love

When it comes to managing the money side of your wedding, be aware that some cutbacks can hurt more than others. Scaling back the hen night, for example, might seem sensible if you need the cash elsewhere. But then what price can you put on the bride's morale? A roller skating session for Sian and her hens sounds like fun, but not when Anna fails to cost in the price of the tickets. 'We could've had six bottles of wine with that,' moans Sian, having covered the entry fee herself. 'I keep thinking it's funny. Then I think, "No, it's not."'

Rian & Matt
The Stag and Hen

What would the world be like without large groups of men parading around the streets dressed as bananas? Nobody does stag and hen dos better (or more ridiculously) than us Brits. Just maybe don't let your other half arrange it for you...

Matt and Rian – The second chancers

'When Matt finally got me to to sit still and he popped the question, I couldn't believe it...'

Rian and Matt were 20 and 16 when they first started dating, but when her work ambitions took her from away from their hometown of Abergavenny it looked as though it was game over for the couple. 'We dated for a couple of months and I was older than him so yes, I'm a cougar!' Rian laughs. 'Then I moved away and lived in Birmingham and London. I came back to see family and friends one weekend, ended up at a beer festival and Matt happened to be there. He asked me out. Our first date was at a car boot sale where we ate our lunch from a burger van and we've barely left each other's sides ever since. I took redundancy from my job in London, moved back to Abergavenny and we moved in together almost straight away.'

Matt proposed 18 months later on Christmas Day in front of Rian's friends and family. She says he couldn't have chosen a better way to do it. 'I had always wanted it to happen in front of the people I'm closest to but I really wasn't expecting it. I'd been necking champagne all day so I was milling around chatting to people and having fun. When Matt finally got me to sit still and he popped the question, I couldn't believe it. I was like "shut up!" He had a speech planned and everything – it was so nice. Matt is not

at all romantic so I did not want him to take me to Venice or the Eiffel Tower or anything because I would have seen the proposal coming, so it was great that he asked me in the way he did.'

Taking a gamble

'Rian didn't trust me at all so I went out of my way to prove that I could do it. I wanted to show her how much I loved her.'

Christmas was barely over before pharmaceutical rep Rian sent off her application form to *Don't Tell The Bride*, and before they knew it they were setting a date. 'It was a proper whirlwind,' recalls Rian. 'We were engaged and married within four months. We had an engagement party in the February and I fell pregnant that night. We found out just before we started filming so there was a lot going on.'

Matt, who manages a residential care home for young people, soon set about making arrangements for the big do. And the confident chap was certain it would be smooth sailing all the way. 'My family thought I was mad but my friends thought it would be a good laugh so they offered to help out. It wasn't until the first day I realised what a huge task it was going to be. I thought it was going to be pretty easy but actually I felt like I was under massive pressure, especially as Rian is such a perfectionist. She really cares about the aesthetics of things, whereas I don't so much. Rian didn't trust me at all so I went out of my way to prove that I could do it. I wanted to show her how much I loved her. And actually it all came together really well and we had an incredible day.'

'Matt decided to treat himself... To *five days* in Las Vegas!'

Vegas, baby

The stag and hen dos are seen as the final 'hurrahs' before you get that ring on your finger and settle down into marital bliss. Whether you choose to spend a weekend in the bars of Dublin or a night down your local, you need to make it memorable. Traditionally it's the job of the best man or maid of honour to do the organising, but while back in the day all details were kept secret from the bride and groom, nowadays it's not unusual for them to have a say in what they'd like to do.

As he was in charge of every aspect of the wedding, Matt also got to decide how he and Rian would enjoy their 'last night of freedom'. And much to Rian's horror, as he also had full control of the budget, he decided to treat himself. To five days in Las Vegas. 'My stag do was brilliant. It wasn't cheap and it ended up costing me about £2,300, but it was brilliant. I was a bit gutted I couldn't afford to take more of my friends with me, but if I had done I would have ended up spending pretty much all of my wedding budget. I was always going to go to Vegas no matter what happened. I didn't tell Rian because she probably wouldn't have let me go so I kept it quiet. There were moments when I

felt really guilty but I didn't let it spoil the enjoyment of it all too much.'

'My hen do wasn't so good,' says Rian, completely deadpan. 'Matt arranged for us to play crazy golf and then go to bingo, both of which were dreadful. The worst thing was that we got thrown out of the bingo for being too loud. We couldn't even have fun in there. To be fair my hen do wouldn't have been that wild anyway because I was pregnant. There's only so much fun you can have when you can't drink, but there are definitely better things I could have done. A spa weekend would have been nice, or somewhere glamorous like the races. I thought he would at least organise for us to go somewhere fancy so we all had our heels on and we had to change into flats when we realised we were going to be hitting balls around a play park. '

Exactly what – *what?* – was going through Matt's head when he was organising their prospective parties? 'I didn't think there was any point in wasting a lot of money on Rian's friends when she was pregnant and couldn't really enjoy herself,' he says, perhaps a little too honestly. 'Also I ran out of money for the hen do after I'd paid for Vegas, and I didn't organise it until a few hours before we got on the plane so I had to keep it simple. I thought it would be funny to send Rian to crazy golf because she always moans about me going off and playing proper golf, but I could have been a bit more generous. I only gave them £100 spending money between 16 of them so that wouldn't have bought them a lot of drinks.'

Rian says the one saving grace was that she had so many of her nearest and dearest around her. 'Loads of my friends came to my hen do whereas Matt only took three of his mates away with him. I think if you want all of your friends on your stag or hen you have to sacrifice going away because not everyone will be able to afford it.

'I loved my wedding but my one regret is that I didn't have a very good hen. I am

planning to have a weekend away with all of my friends soon though, so that will make up for it. I think it's so important to do something spectacular when you're saying goodbye to your single life. My hen do will definitely be memorable – just for the wrong reasons.'

Having learned from her slightly disappointing experience, Rian says that when it comes to organising her second bash Matt won't get a look in. 'He got to party for five days, my friends got to drink watered down Sex on the Beach cocktails. He spent 20 percent of the budget on his stag do and £100 on the hen do, so he definitely won't get a say in anything I arrange this time. I know he secretly feels guilty about going to Vegas and I wish he wouldn't because I really wanted him to enjoy it, and once it's done it's done. At the end of the day I think you have to do what you want so I can't really blame him.'

Flyover hangover

'All I wanted to do was sleep but I had to film the show, and of course I had to carry on planning the wedding...'

Her sedate hen do and pregnancy meant that Rian woke up the following morning hangover free. But it was a very different story for Matt. Despite planning to party like it's 1999 (well, 2013) it seems there's only so much Vegas a man can take. 'We arrived at 7pm on the first night and didn't go to bed until 6am, then we were up at 8.30am for filming. Our hangovers were horrendous but we didn't really have time to indulge them because we were so busy. We did go over the top with the drinking at times so we had to take a bit of time out now and again. All of us ended up staying in at least one of nights. One of the lads spent 30 hours in bed. He literally couldn't move because he was such a mess. I felt like I was being punished some days because all I wanted to do was sleep but I had to film the show, and of course I had to carry on planning the wedding. There were some points where I ended up lying on the floor in hotel reception because I was such a mess. It was a combination of jetlag and hangover. So many funny things happened on that trip though. My mates made me go out in "I love TOWIE" knickers one night, and they also dressed me up as a woman. It was a typical stupid, drunken stag do.'

Matt may have had the stag do of his dreams, but he also experienced the return journey from hell after he messed up the group's flight schedule, meaning he was left feeling tired, panicked and with little time to plan the rest of the wedding. 'It took us two days to get home in total. We had to travel from Vegas to Orlando, wait for twelve hours there, then fly to New York, and then go from New York to Heathrow. I reckon that was my penance for having such a good time. By the time I got back I only had two weeks to arrange everything, which didn't turn out to be very long. If I learnt anything from my stag do it's to check your travel times. Then check them again.'

If you and your mates are planning a stag or hen do, here are some tips to make it run more smoothly (take note, Matt):

- **Give people plenty of notice and let them know what kind of bash it's going to be so they can start planning their outfit/source any fancy dress clothes or stag and hen paraphernalia.**
- **Stick to a budget.**
- **Arrange something everyone can enjoy, especially if you've got lots of different age groups coming.**
- **Be realistic about timings, and if you're going to more than one venue arrange transport to ferry everyone around quickly and easily.**
- **Give everyone a printout with details of the day, including the address of every place you're visiting, details of the last trains and buses home and local taxi numbers.**
- **Remember that not everyone has pots of cash. Allow people to dip in and out of certain parts of the day. For instance, if you plan to go for dinner and then to a club, some people may wish to skip the meal and meet you at the club.**
- **Do a whip round for those drinking to make bar runs easier. If people are staying alcohol-free, allow them to buy their own drinks if they'd prefer.**
- **If you're planning to head further afield like Matt, make sure the place you're visiting welcomes stag and hen parties (some hotels and rental properties have a strict ban).**
- **If you're planning a night out in a smart club don't forget that, unlike the UK where pretty much anything goes, a lot of swish places abroad don't let people in if they're wearing trainers, shorts, fancy dress or anything *too* revealing (Matt admits he got refused entry to one club while he was dressed as a woman. Can't imagine why).**

Rian and Matt are now very proud parents to their daughter, Mali, and two years on Rian has found it in her heart to forgive Matt for the hen do disaster. 'He did such a good job of the wedding that I can definitely excuse the hen do let down,' Rian smiles. 'Matt was so thoughtful and I loved everything about the actual day. Well, apart from the rings. He bought us both exactly the same ones so mine was also a massive man's ring. It wouldn't even fit on my thumb. He wanted us to have matching rings, which was a nice sentiment, but I genuinely think the ones he chose were actually for a gay wedding. But overall, things were just brilliant and it was a really special time in my life. I got married on TV, had a baby and celebrated my 30th birthday all in one year. I'm not sure how I can ever top that!'

Highlights from the Show... The Stag and Hen Experience

Katie and Darnell – Unlucky for some

It's Katie's last ever night out as a single lady. Together with her friends, she's all dressed up and ready to go on the razzle. Leaving fiancé, Darnell, to organise a night she'll never forget, our bride and her happy hens find themselves sipping champagne as a chauffeur-driven pink Hummer escorts them all the way… to the local bingo hall. Meanwhile, Darnell makes up for their lack of fun by living it large on his stag night. 'It's like bringing someone all the way up the roof of the Hilton,' Katie observes bitterly as her numbers fail to deliver, 'and then kicking them off the top.'

Ellie and Craig – The no expense spent hen night

Battling to deliver a dream wedding on budget, Craig is forced to make drastic cutbacks. When Ellie and her friends receive a text with instructions for her hen night, their initial response is high excitement. A special area reserved at a West End nightclub with drinks and nibbles laid on? Somehow, it seems that Craig has seriously pushed the boat out. Then Ellie discovers that they're expected to foot the bill for the long, arduous journey into London – the equivalent of being asked to supply her own oars. Several hours later with a tired nan in tow, the party arrive to discover Craig has put just £100 behind the bar. How the hens laughed! Actually, they didn't.

Tom and Lottie – Sad song

'What we're going to do here today,' beams the bespectacled entertainer laid on by Tom for Lottie's hen party, 'is sing some songs!' As tumbleweed moments go, the silence speaks volumes before Lottie heads for the exit. 'He really doesn't know me at all, does he?' she says, before returning to the fold of her friends and bursting into tears. Across town, our groom is having what might be a wasted haircut while looking very pleased with himself. 'She does love the attention a little bit,' he says confidently. 'I think she'll be alright.'

Anthony and Holly – Nerd is the word

Science geek Anthony has a treat in store for bride Holly and her assembled hens. Will it be a night on the tiles with strippers, drinking, dancing and debauchery? Presented with a video message from the groom himself, along with a mystery box, the girls are invited to extract the contents and let the party begin. 'If you'll just put your lab coats on, and your goggles,' he begins, as Holly and co struggle to express their excitement. 'Does this make you want to marry him more or less?' asks one hen as Anthony introduces the first of the evening's experiments. Holly considers the question for a nanosecond. 'Categorically,' she declares, 'I'm saying less!'

Ian and Jay – Hen dos and don'ts

Having flown all the way to Thailand with his mates in a bid to buy a cheap wedding dress, Ian decides it would be rude not to stage a stag do while he's there. Sure enough, a night out in Bangkok sees the lads have the time of their lives. Meanwhile, back home on a wet and windswept hillside, Jay and the girls struggle to make the most of Ian's treat – an afternoon of zorbing. 'I'm so glad I spent four hours doing my hair this morning,' says one hen, bitterly, 'to be chucked down the hill in a ball.'

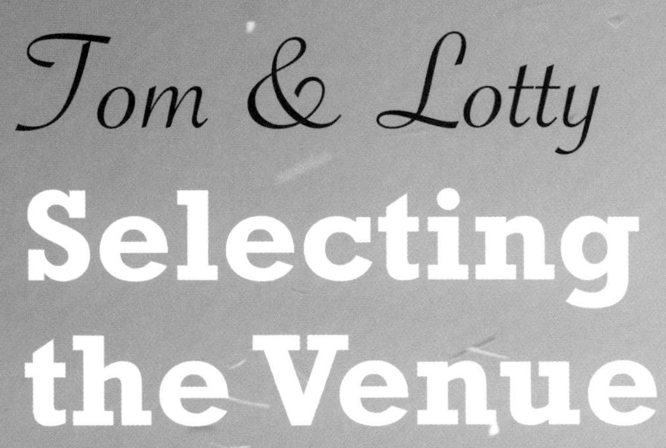

Tom & Lotty
Selecting the Venue

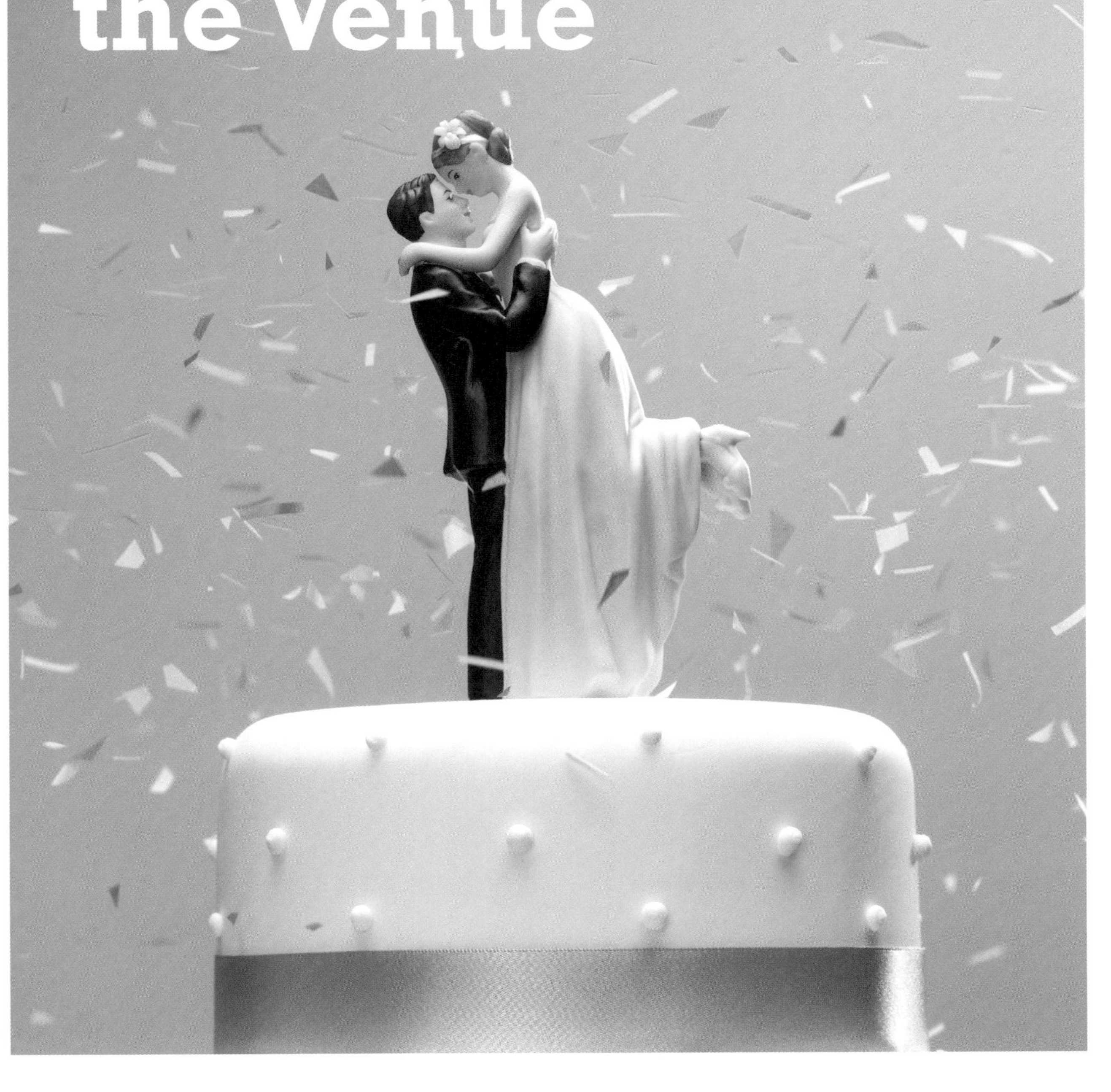

From tree houses to aquariums, couples can get married pretty much anywhere these days. So what's stopping you living out your wildest fantasies on the biggest day of your life? While not all venues come with a marriage licence, most will be suitable for non-legal blessings and parties, so the sky is quite literally the limit (hot air balloon anyone?).

Tom and Lotty – The accidental lovebirds

'A zoo, a museum, a lighthouse, a castle, a pub... The choice is yours.'

Bricklayer Tom and insurance broker Lotty first met on a drunken night out in their hometown of Bristol. But it wasn't until a year later that they finally got together. Er, by mistake. 'Lotty meant to text her nephew, who is also called Tom, but she mixed up our numbers, so she ended up texting her future husband instead!' laughs Tom. 'We went to "Henry Africas" in town for drinks for our first date and I fell in love with her as soon as I saw her. We had a great night and we got on so well it all kind of fell into place.

'I'd sworn myself off men and I hadn't planned to meet, marry or have kids with anyone for at least five years so I wasn't looking at all. Then Tom came along,' Lotty adds. 'He won me over and in the end it took him five years to propose so it all worked out perfectly.'

Tom finally popped the question on his birthday, 30th June 2009, at Bristol's Brasserie Blanc. He chose the restaurant because his and Lotty's parents both got married in the nearby registry office. The proposal came completely out of the blue for Lotty, but once she said 'yes' it was fast forward all the way. 'I had no idea whatsoever he was going to ask me to marry him but I was very happy when he did. We had a very busy 13 months. We got engaged in June 2009, bought a flat the same year, married in June 2010, and then I fell pregnant two weeks later. We now have two boys – Samuel, four, and Elliott, 18 months. We certainly didn't waste any time!'

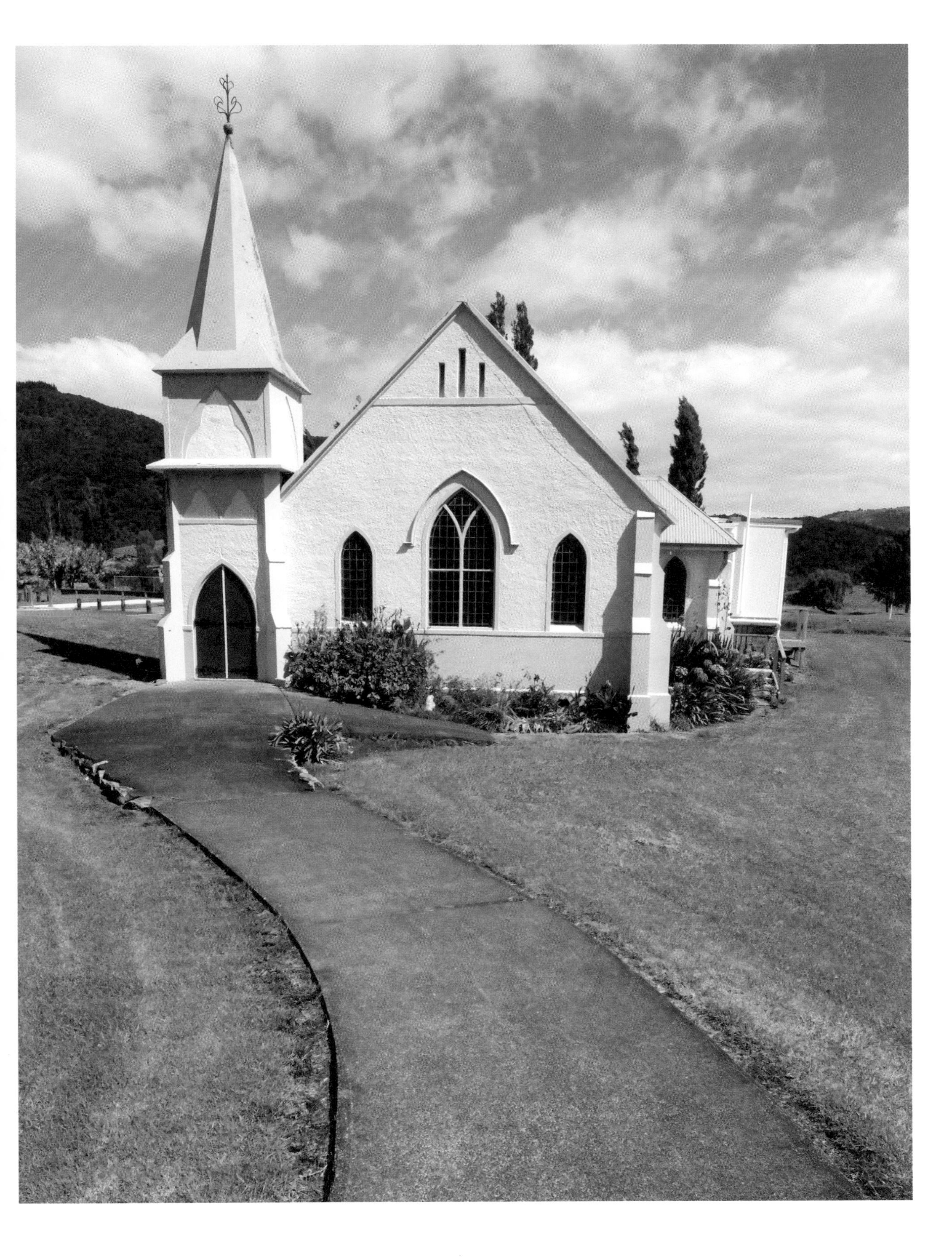

Milling around

'The worst place he could have booked was somewhere water-based or involving fast rides...'

Lotty admits that metrosexual Tom was the perfect person to plan their wedding. And despite her nerves, everything ran relatively smoothly. He chose a beautiful church for the wedding ceremony, knowing just how much it would mean to Lotty. 'I knew I wanted that church in particular above everything else. Lotty's mum died when she was young and her funeral was held at the church, so she's got a massive connection to it. Before the show she hadn't been back inside the church for 22 years and I know it meant everything to her to be walking up that aisle.'

Tom wanted to have a big outside element to the reception so he booked Prinston Mill in Bath, which boasts beautiful grounds. But he did have to compromise on some elements of his plan. 'Reception wise, I wanted Mongolian tents but the budget wouldn't stretch to

'There's little point in getting married at the top of a mountain if half your relatives won't be able to make it up there.'

them so I had to let that go. But it meant I could incorporate things that I knew Lotty would like, such as a barbershop quartet, and all in all I was really happy with it.'

Lotty was more than happy with his choices. 'I'm a traditionalist and I love all of the pomp and ceremony, and the church was perfect for me. I was kind of hoping the reception would be in a stately home but I had no idea where Tom would pick. I wouldn't have been at all surprised if he'd kept things simple and gone for a church hall, and because he loves surfing I also envisaged myself sat on a beach eating fish and chips. I'd never heard of Prinston Mill before. It was a beautiful, disused mill, and a small, quaint period building, which was lovely. I was really pleased when I saw it. The worst place he could have booked was somewhere water-based or involving fast rides because I have a bit of a phobia of both. I really felt for the woman who did the skydive in one of the episodes of *Don't Tell The Bride* because that would have been my idea of hell.'

Location, Location, Location

A zoo, a museum, a lighthouse, a castle, a pub… The choice is yours. It's a good plan to have a firm idea of the kind of venue you're after before you start looking around. Time is of the essence when you're planning a wedding so narrow your choices down to no more than ten locations and visit the ones at the top of your list first.

If you're happy to have a very small ceremony most places will be suitable, so you need to decide how important it is for you have to lots of people there.

Other key things to consider:

- **Is the venue easily accessible?**
- **Is there room for everyone to stay?**
- **Do you have permission to marry at your chosen place?**
- **How many toilets are available?**
- **Is there a room where the bride and bridesmaids can have some privacy to touch up their make-up/get changed for the evening?**
- **Is there a separate bar area?**
- **Does the venue have an alcohol licence?**
- **Can you do bring your own alcohol?**
- **Is there outside space?**
- **Can you go to the venue the day before the wedding to check everything is as it should be?**
- **Do they have a PA system?**
- **Do they have a projector in case it's needed for the speeches?**
- **Is confetti allowed?**
- **What time do they close/expect you to be out of the venue?**

Lotty is relieved Tom took a chance and didn't opt for a standard hotel wedding because it would have felt too much like being back at work. 'I've been to a lot of weddings in hotels and personally I find some of them a bit soulless, but that's probably because I go to a lot of conferences in hotels through my work. I would have hated to have been somewhere where I looked around at the flowery wallpaper and it felt like Groundhog Day. Of course I think our wedding was the best ever because everyone does, but I have been to some other really nice ones. Some friends of ours had this wedding in quite an industrial setting, which you may think would be weird, but it looked stylish and quirky. They had candles in jam jars on strings and it was very urban.'

Most people love a good boogie at a wedding, but not everyone enjoys blaring music and some guests may crave a quiet chat with their friends and family. It's always good to have a space away from

the dance floor so people can escape if it gets too noisy for them. 'I think the best thing you could do when you're choosing a wedding reception is have somewhere that has lots of levels and spaces. I loved the fact that people could hang out in different places and go where they wanted. I've been to weddings where you have no choice but to be in the dance area, which isn't great if you want to have a chat with someone. You can't organise other people's fun and people like a choice. At our wedding, people could go in the dance floor area if they wanted, or they could go to the bar if they wanted a pint and a chat, or if they had kids they could go and sit on the grass outside. Tom and I were able to wander around all of those different areas and chat to our guests. It was so nice.'

Bag a bargain

'Since there is less demand, winter weddings generally work out cheaper than summer ones.'

Budget is a huge factor in your choice of setting. Venues can cost anything from £100 to £100,000, so before you get carried away be realistic about what you can afford. Are family going to be helping you out? If you splash out on an amazing location will you have to compromise on everything else? If your wedding is a long way off you could set up a separate bank account and pay a certain amount of your wages in each month so you can build up a good fund. This will definitely give you a bit more freedom with your choices.

Since there is less demand, winter weddings generally work out cheaper than summer ones. If you're determined to save money, get married midweek when venues are less in demand, and therefore cost a lot less. Even Fridays and Sundays can work out a lot more reasonable. But bear in mind that some guests may not be able to take time off work so prepare yourself for people declining your kind invitation if you have it on a weekday (although this is a good way to keep numbers down!).

You could even hold the ceremony in your own/a friend's/family member's house/garden if you want to avoid a huge bill. If you do decide to go for a garden or marquee wedding here are some key things to think about:

- **Chair, table hire and heater hire**
- **Portaloo/luxury toilet hire (inside toilets are rarely sufficient if you have a large number of guests)**
- **Where will people dance?**
- **Do you need to hire a dance floor?**
- **Are electrics available?**
- **Will you have hot or cold food? (You could hire a food van)**
- **Are there enough parking facilities?**

Pubs and church halls can be hired for next to nothing. Because they often only charge around £100 a night for the whole place (some pubs and bars will let you have it for free if you can guarantee a certain amount will be taken behind the bar) they tend to get very booked up. So if you like the idea of keeping things down to earth make sure you secure it well in advance.

Quality or quantity?

'At the end of the day what you want is a group of people in one place having a good time, and that can be anywhere you choose.'

Needless to say, if you have a small do you will have extra money to make it a lot more lavish. For instance, you could probably host dinner for ten at The Ritz for the same price as a 100-seater event at a more modest hotel. It all depends on what kind of day you want to have. It's important to estimate the cost per head and work from that figure.

Hotels often offer package deals that can shave a fortune off the cost of your day. If you want to know that everything from the seat covers to the carnations are covered, this is the way to go.

Don't be afraid to negotiate (reduced room rates for guests is a must) and do read the contract before you agree to everything because sometimes there can be hidden costs you're not expecting, such as VAT, cloakroom fees, hire of a PA system or corkage.

Tom has some sound pearls of wisdom when it comes to cutting costs and planning your day. 'If I could give someone who's planning a wedding a bit of advice, it would be to keep the fact it's a wedding quiet. The minute you mention that word, the price of everything rockets, so try and pretend it's a birthday party or something and you won't get ripped off. Also, stick with your ideas and don't be put off by what other people say because things that may seem a bit dubious can turn out to be absolutely fantastic. Have confidence in your own ability because when doubt starts creeping in you may feel like changing your mind about a really good idea and then regret it. At the end of the day what you want is a group of people in one place having a good time, and that can be anywhere you choose. We had a brilliant wedding. We were very, very lucky.'

Highlights from the Show... Selecting the Venue

Hollie and James – The rooftop Romeo

Selecting the perfect location for your wedding can take some imagination. James pushes this to the limit by inviting his best man, Tom, to visit his first choice of venue: a multi-storey car park in Peckham. 'I love the idea of taking something really dark, dingy and horrible,' he says dreamily as they enter a stairwell reeking of wee, 'and turning it into this amazing, spectacular environment.' Meanwhile, Hollie tortures herself by visiting the picture postcard church where several generations of her family have celebrated their marriage. 'Shall I just walk down the aisle?' she suggests to her sisters with a note of resignation, 'in case I don't get that chance?'

Noel and Jemma – The Magaluf marriage

When a holiday in Magaluf ended in disappointment for Noel and Jemma, only one of them wisely assumed they'd never return. For Noel, a crap break becomes a challenge, and persuades him to stage their wedding on the holiday isle. 'It's the biggest gamble ever,' he says breezily, with no idea that the odds would begin to stack against him. As for Jemma, blissfully unaware of the plans, she leaves Noel with simple, but ominous words of advice. 'Don't let me down,' she says, leaving our groom with no option but to chuckle nervously.

Rosie and Dave – The lambing shed

Dave has arrived on the island of Lundy. It's remote, rugged and notably short of venues for a wedding reception. Together with his two best mates, Tonky and Spew, he's come to check out the only structure that might just house his guests. Yes, it's a lambing shed, but Dave can see beyond all the hay and the muck. His friends, however, are more pragmatic. 'Don't be ridiculous!' Spew scoffs. 'Look at it!' adds Tonky, while looking at Dave in disbelief. Despite the response, our groom won't give up. 'But if worst came to worst, we could use this, couldn't we?' The boys draw breath between their teeth and encourage Dave back out into the open air.

Mike and Katie – The high life

Mike goes in search of a wedding venue for his bride, Katie. Knowing how much she likes the high life, he pays a visit to Blackpool Tower. Gathering in the lift with the boys, ready to rocket to the top, the groom is certain he's found the perfect place. Then the lift begins its swift ascent, and Mike's confidence starts to deserts him. 'I'm alright so far,' he says shakily as they head upwards. 'OOH, not any more. Not any more!' In the end, Mike opts to keep his feet on the ground and weds Katie at the town's equally iconic Winter Gardens.

Nick and Vicky – In the dark

The groom believes he's found the ideal location to tie the knot. Yes, it's a working farm, but the place is licenced to hold wedding ceremonies. Together with his brothers, Nick gathers around the raised, circular stage inside the farm's marquee and pictures the happy moment. There might be a striking lack of natural light, but in his mind it's shining brightly. 'I like it dark,' he declares with confidence, unaware that his bride is away discussing her hopes and dreams. 'I'd go mad if it was inside and dark,' says Vicky. 'I really would.'

Levi & Jade

Fabulous Themes and Broken Dreams

Behind every good wedding is a basic template. The bride and groom exchange their vows at a ceremony, before invited guests toast the couple's future at a reception event. All sorts of customs, rituals and traditions can influence and shape things, but often the challenge lies in personalising the day.

It's only natural to want your wedding to be meaningful, and feel like it belongs to you both. It's a celebration of your new life together, after all. While some seek to tweak the traditional way of getting hitched, and tailor it to suit their tastes, increasingly couples look to frame their day with a theme.

We could be talking about anything here from a single concept to a complex idea. Quite literally, you can make what you want of it, and the world is your oyster. Whether you choose to simply highlight a signature colour or recreate a historical era down to the tiniest detail, the role of a theme in your wedding can be as low key or as grand as you like. So what's the draw, and how can you be sure that your efforts will transform a wedding into a day that people remember for all the right reasons?

Levi and Jade – The stadium filler

'Despite her dreams of a traditional, vintage wedding, he turned to another love of his life for inspiration: football – the beautiful game not generally known for its huge bridal fan base.'

When Jade agreed to let fiancé Levi handle plans for their wedding, she figured his love of music would play a central role in the day. 'I met Levi when we were kids at school, so we've known each other for ages,' she says. 'He's always been passionate about rock and roll, and admires stars

like Liam Gallagher. I just thought that was the kind of thing he'd turn to for inspiration.'

The Stoke-on-Trent couple might appear to make an unlikely match, but they're clearly besotted with each other. A former bad boy, with a cheeky smile and a swagger, Levi is first to admit that level-headed Jade, the daughter of a military man, rescued him from his previous life. 'I was definitely a rebel,' he says. 'Knocking about on the streets with the lads; clubbing, drinking and just having a laugh. Then I got together with Jade, and she pulled me onto the right path,' he admits. 'Being with her, I realised that if I put my mind to things and worked hard I could do whatever I wanted.'

It was this newfound outlook that led Levi to think big for his wedding theme. 'I wanted to step up and repay her,' he explains. 'At the end of the day, she saved me from who I was, and I wanted to make her proud of me. I was also confident that I could organise something a lot better than anything she could throw together!'

With an ambition to prove himself, Levi decided that rock and roll just wasn't enough to win over his bride. Despite her dreams of a traditional, vintage wedding, he turned to another love of his life for inspiration: football – the beautiful game not generally known for its huge bridal fan base. As Levi recognised early on, his choice of theme wasn't guaranteed to sweep Jade off her feet. Even so, he firmly believed it would be the perfect way for them to kick off married life together. 'It was just something I've always watched and played,' he explains. 'Jade knows

football is a huge part of who I am. It's a part of my personality and always will be. That gave me the confidence to think I could bring out that passion on such a grand scale that it would take her breath away.'

The dream of a theme

In the right hands, a theme can transform a wedding. Not only is it an expression of your interests and personality – as an individual or a couple – it can invest the day with a sense of fun, style, excitement, drama, delight and sheer originality. From a winter wonderland at the height of summer, to a cowboy western or a space age canteen, your choice could well become a talking point and even a springboard for everyone to shake off their inhibitions and celebrate your union in style.

It doesn't have to be about dressing up, of course, or pushing at boundaries in any sense. A subtle nod to the seasonal style, using little more than flowers and fabrics, could be enough to bring the different elements of your wedding together. It really is down to you, which means you need to be clear from the start what role you wish the theme to play. Naturally, as a couple it's well worth sitting down to work out whether your day will benefit from such customising and to what degree, but there are no rules here. In short, you can go as large or as low key as you like.

Tasked with single-handedly planning their wedding, Levi set out to make his theme literally dominate their day. 'I wanted us to get married on the pitch at Stoke City's stadium,' he says matter-of-factly, 'on a match day in front of a capacity crowd. Everything from the atmosphere to the noise just seemed to fit with what Jade meant to me. I saw it as something that nobody would forget. Especially the people in the area.' Despite initial reservations from his best man, Levi's commitment to his chosen theme didn't once waver. 'It felt right as soon as the thought came into my mind,' he says. 'All I wanted to do was make it a massive, massive wedding that was all for her. From that moment on, I did everything I could to make it happen.'

While Levi's football theme sounds like every boy's dream, rather than a bride with little interest in the game – he insists that his aim was to demonstrate to Jade just how much she meant to him. 'I wanted her to realise how far I'd go to make our wedding special,' he says. 'I basically approached the whole theme with the idea that "the bigger I made it the better." That was all there was to it, and let's be honest you don't get much bigger than a stadium on match day!'

'As well as time and money, your planning skills, and ability to work under pressure can make the difference between disaster and success.'

The goals...

So, you've settled on a theme, but not everyone can share Levi's sheer determination from the start. In short, you need to ask yourself if it's something you can realistically deliver. First and foremost, before picking up the phone to order a squadron of Spitfires to fly over your RAF-style ceremony, you need to be confident that you can afford it. There's nothing more stressful than running out of cash before everything is in place, which is why it's so important to plan every step to be sure you have it covered. What's more, you could be looking at a great deal of time-intensive management to be sure it actually happens. The planes might sound like the perfect way to seal your marriage, but what if it falls to you to seek clearance from air traffic control?

Ultimately, only you can decide if your dream theme isn't going to turn your nuptials into a nightmare. As well as time and money, your planning skills, and ability to work under pressure can make the difference between disaster and success. When Levi first came up with his plan to tie the knot during half time at a Premier League football fixture, his best man openly questioned whether he had bitten off more than he could chew. Compromise might be key in getting some themes up and running, but our groom had no intention of cutting corners. As a project manager by profession, Levi felt sure that he could call upon his experience to stay cool and sleep easy. 'When a client sets out what they want, it's my job to deliver it,' he explains. 'I couldn't afford to settle for second-best, and that single-minded focus helped me to make this wedding happen just as I imagined it. Of course hiccups happen along the way, but you can't let that stop you. Ultimately, everything had to be spot on no matter what.'

...And the glory!

Now a football theme might not be at the top of every bride's wedding wish list. Sure enough, on finding herself presented with the bridal boots on arriving at the stadium, Jade's poker face painted a thousand words. Maybe it was the roar of the crowd that persuaded her on to the pitch, but having taken that brave step Levi's other half now considers it to be a back-of-the-net result she wouldn't change for the world. 'More than anything, I was just so impressed at what he had achieved,' she says, reflecting on the moment that it dawned on her just what Levi had in store for her. 'He'd had this dream, and made it happen, and I just wanted to say to him, "See? You can do stuff if you put your mind to it!" I'd always thought that I did far too much for him, and this proved how capable he could be when left to his own devices!'

As for Levi, he believes it was the little details that ensured his big theme connected with his new bride. 'I'm well aware that football said a great deal about me rather than her. I also confess that I hoped it would get my future father-in-law onside because he's a massive Stoke City fan, but everything else that went into it was for Jade. The scale of the event was one thing, but I knew the finishing touches would be equally important, if not more, and that was uppermost in my mind every step of the way. From the bridesmaids' outfits to her dress, the flowers, the transport, the reception event and the cake design, I wanted her to feel at the centre of it all.

'It was a massive undertaking,' he continues, 'and I was still in planning mode throughout the day. Waiting for Jade in the players' tunnel, I was thinking ahead to the reception and ticking off all these to-do boxes in my mind. At the same time, as soon as I set eyes on Jade – and don't forget we hadn't seen each other for three weeks – I knew my efforts had paid off. Straight away, I felt this great weight lift from my shoulders. Just being together again, as we stepped out onto the pitch in front of all those people, it actually felt like we were at home.'

STOKE CITY
THE POTTERS

The post-~~match~~ wedding analysis

> **'Big or little, a theme has to say something about you, individually or as a couple, but also what the wedding means to you both.'**

Looking back, Jade recognises that Levi's unwavering approach to creating a wedding with a huge theme worked wonders. 'It was a crazy idea based on his lifelong passion for the game,' she says, 'but because I know him so well I understood his reasons behind it. In many ways, recognising that is what gave me the most perfect day. And yes,' she adds, 'even my dad was proud of his achievements!'

Without doubt, a theme can help to focus the day, and bring your interests, tastes or passions to the fore, but is there a risk that it dominates proceedings, or even overwhelms? While Jade and Levi chose to mark their marriage by going extra-large, the couple maintain that it isn't the scale of your ambitions that count here. Essentially, it's the commitment and effort behind it. 'My heart and soul went into making that day feel special,' says Levi. 'You can't just write out a cheque for that to happen. Big or little, a theme has to say something about you, individually or as a couple, but also what the wedding means to you both.'

With plans to return to the stadium for a forthcoming anniversary, and a baby son recently added to the team sheet, Jade has no regrets about her new-found fame as the football bride. 'People remember it, and talk about it all the time, but at the end of the day it was all about a marriage. We might've been married in front of thousands, but despite the scale of the day it was still about two people pledging their love and commitment to each other. Even if we'd gone down the traditional route, Levi and I would still be just as happy as we are now, and that's what really matters.'

Alex & Kara

An Invitation to the Wedding

We all love that moment when a crisp white envelope drops onto our doormat inviting us to someone's nuptials. A wedding invite sets the tone for the day and lets guests know what to expect. But you don't necessarily have to go for the conventional card-style invites. As long as all of the important information is included you have free rein to get creative.

Alex and Kara – The festival flames

Music lovers Alex and Kara met through friends, and a year and a half later, a drunken Alex knelt down in a muddy field and popped the question. 'Kara and I first met in a nightclub in Reading, where we're both from, when I was 21 and Kara was 24. We got introduced through mutual friends and I ended up asking her out. We went to Go Ape on our first date and then we started going to gigs together because we both love music. I proposed at Reading Festival after we'd been together for a year and a half. A band called The Phoenix were playing and I got down on one knee and asked her. Thankfully she said yes straight away.'

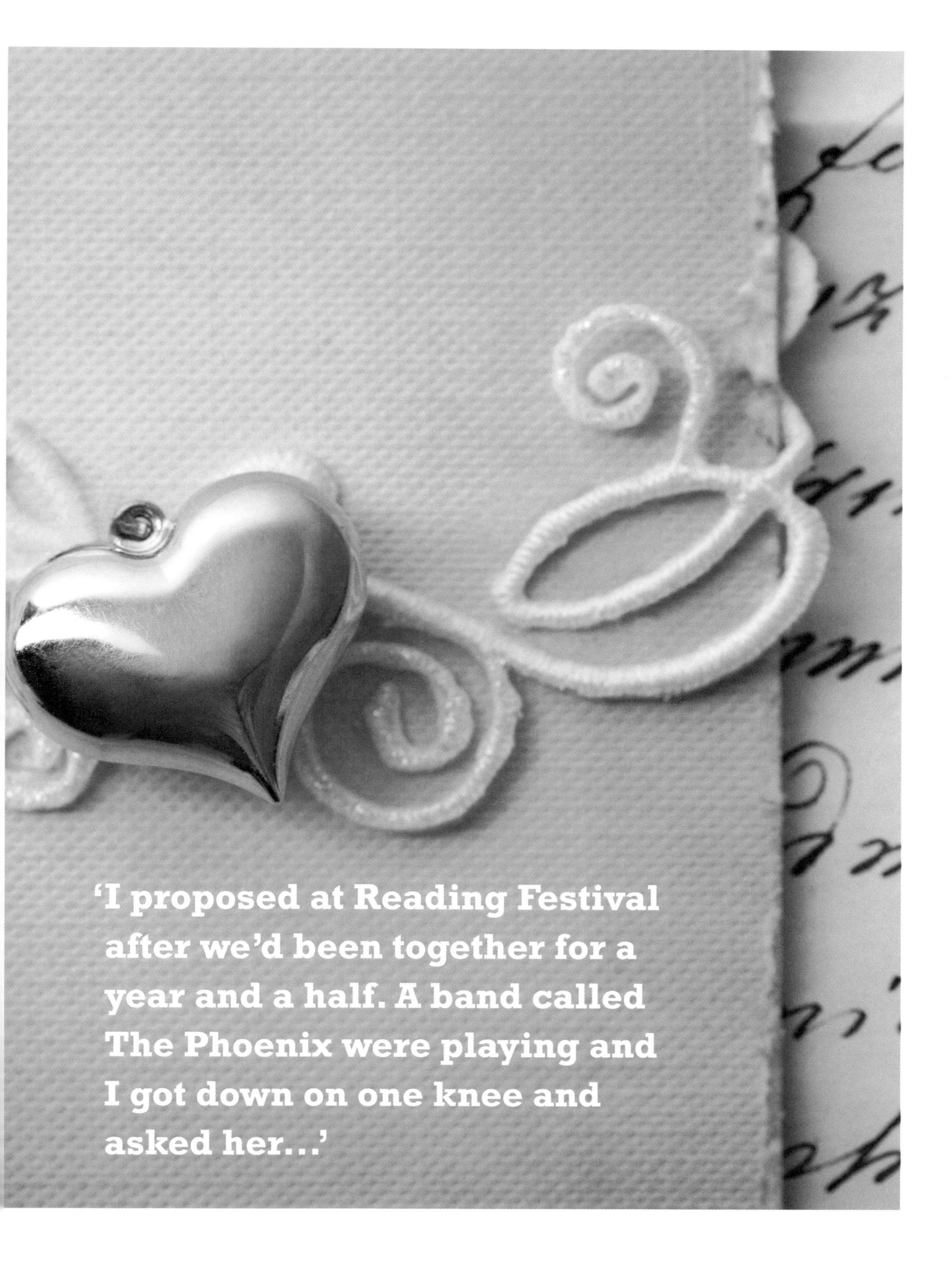
'I proposed at Reading Festival after we'd been together for a year and a half. A band called The Phoenix were playing and I got down on one knee and asked her...'

It certainly wasn't love at first sight for Kara, but now she couldn't imagine being without her skateboard-mad husband. 'I didn't really like Alex at first if I'm being completely honest. I thought he was a bit of a ladies' man but our first date was so much fun he won me over. He wasn't who I thought he was and after that we spent a lot more time together. We were surrounded by thousands of people when he proposed but it was like we were in our own little world. It was hilarious because we were both very drunk, but that's not the only reason I said "yes". I already knew I wanted to marry him.'

Alex and Kara are always up for trying something a bit different, and *Don't Tell The Bride* seemed like the perfect way for them to do just that. 'We sent off an application form and a few photos, and when we got a call saying we'd been accepted we were well happy. I thought it was cool to have all of the control over the wedding because Kara's a bit of a control freak. It was pretty stressful every now and again but I actually got really into it and had a good laugh.'

Hair stylist Kara, meanwhile, had mixed feelings about Alex taking charge. 'Letting Alex plan the wedding was like a catch 22. Part of me thought it was a good idea because it meant I didn't have to do it myself and get stressed. But then I got stressed because he was doing it!'

I believe in fête

'Because it was in a field there was no cut-off point. It meant everyone just carried on partying, so we definitely made the most of it.'

Alex pulled together an amazing summer fête-themed day at Lilibrooke Manor in Maidenhead. It included a bouncy castle, coconut shy and rodeo bull, and he even arranged for Kara to arrive in an ice-cream van.

'Even though I didn't get to choose my own dress or anything I still felt fantastic when I walked up the aisle,' says Kara. 'I was really happy with everything Alex did. I wanted people to come away from our wedding thinking they'd never been to anything like it and I reckon it was job done. It was a very long day because it started at 10am and didn't end until 4am the following morning, but I loved every minute of it. Because it was in a field there was no cut-off point. It meant everyone just carried on partying, so we definitely made the most of it.'

In keeping with his quirky take on things, Alex also ensured Kara had a rather unusual (and very personal) invite to the big day. 'I sent her a note on the day of her hen do saying that she had to do something completely on her own and that one of my best men, Jack, was going to pick her up. She was terrified because she immediately thought she'd have to go on Jack's motorbike and she hates them, but I wouldn't have done that to her. Jack is a tattoo artist and I thought if she got a tattoo of our wedding date it would be a good way for her to remember the day forever. There was a small chance she would have said she didn't want it, but in the back of my mind I knew she would be okay. I've also had a tattoo done since the wedding. I don't wear any jewellery so I've got a 'K' on my wedding finger instead of a ring.'

So did Kara have any reservations about having a permanent reminder of the all-important date inked onto on her left calf? 'Having the tattoo was actually a relief because I was physically sick when I thought the surprise was going on the back of Jack's Harley Davidson. I have a real fear of motorbikes so there's no way I would have done it. When I read Jack's note saying I was finding out the date of the wedding by having it tattooed on me I actually felt really happy because it meant I finally got to find out when I was getting married. Alex was the one who suggested that I have the tattoo on my leg and I liked the place he chose. I could easily have said no if I'd wanted to but it didn't even cross my mind. I liked the fact the tattoo was in Roman numerals too. Some people may hate it but it suited me. It was definitely an unusual invite. But having said that it's not that unusual for Alex. The only problem is I have no excuse when I forget our wedding anniversary which, believe it or not, I still do!'

Get crafty

Invites can take all manner of different forms, from take-away boxes to video messages, a VIP-style lanyard, or you could even have the details printed onto a chocolate wrapper. However you wish to do it, it should be in keeping with your colour scheme and theme and have all the information everyone needs, including the gift list.

- **You're potentially going to have to make a large number so keep the design simple. Also use minimal embellishments, or your invites could end up being more expensive than the shop-bought equivalent.**

- **If you're bulk-buying embellishments from Ebay, check the delivery date carefully. A lot of products come from abroad and some state (not always that obviously) that they can take up to two months to arrive.**

- **If you're in any doubt about a product ask to see a sample. Things often look very different up close than they do on the internet and you don't want to order giant powder blue flowers only to discover they're actually light purple.**

- **Consider printer costs. Home printer cartridges cost a small fortune, so it may be more cost savvy to get a local printer to do them for you.**

- **The font you choose is really important and can say everything – or nothing! If you choose a fancy squiggly font, it can be hard to read when it's printed onto certain papers, so it's best to do a test run by printing something at home first.**

- **Mock up a dummy invite before you go ahead and make them all. You may well spot something you're not happy with, and it's better to do that early on.**

Wheelie bad

'Make sure you get a comprehensive guest list from your bride's family. And send out the invites as soon as you can!'

It would have been a little ambitious (not to mention costly and time consuming) for Alex to tattoo the date of the wedding onto all of the guests' legs, so he opted for something more straightforward when it came to everyone else's invites. 'Handily a friend of ours owns a printing company so I got her to make some up for me,' explains Alex. 'I drew out a design and she transformed it into an invite. They were all white with black writing and every line was in a different font, then on the back it was black with white writing. I gave Kara her own invite in the shape of a skateboard just to annoy her. I knew she would think I was either organising a skateboard-themed wedding, or I was an idiot, and I wanted her to think it was a skateboard wedding. Obviously it was the latter and she did cotton on pretty quickly. I would never have gone for a traditional invite because it's not the sort of thing Kara and I like, and I was really pleased with how mine turned out.'

Alex even managed to impress Kara with his sleek design. However, he didn't get everything right… 'The invites Alex chose were really, really nice, but he did forget to invite quite a lot of people, including my auntie, my uncle and my cousins. All of our friends knew about the wedding through Facebook so they turned up, but not all of my family are on social media so they didn't know the details. As a result they didn't think they were invited. So Alex did really well with the design of the invites, but not actually sending them out to people. The ones he did give out he delivered a few days before the actual day. He had so much stuff to do it must have slipped his mind. The invite he sent me was exactly the same design as everyone else's but it was in the shape of a skateboard because he thought it would be funny to try and mess with my head. It was so tacky and horrible, and I knew he'd think it was funny. There

'We had our place cards and thank you cards made by the same friend who did our invites so they all matched nicely.'

was a fleeting moment when I thought he'd sent them to everyone – well, those he'd remembered – and I was so cross because it would have been ridiculous.'

Alex admits he did leave sending out the invites slightly to the last minute, and funnily enough he would advise other people against it! 'I delivered all of the invites I could in one evening. Jack and I jumped in his car and put them through people's letterboxes, and I sent some others through normal post. As Kara mentioned, I missed out loads of people. In my defence, I did ask her mum to invite everyone from her family but our wires got crossed, so she only invited the immediate family. If I had a chance to do it again I would definitely organise things differently. And would say to any guys who are planning a wedding on behalf of their bride, if you want to make sure everyone is going to turn up send out the invites as soon as you can!'

Be 'Appy

These days, people often save money by inviting friends and family via social media – a message on Facebook, a photo on Instagram or even a straight to the point tweet all do the job. However, be aware that people don't always treat those kind of invites with the same respect as they do a paper one, and it can also be hard to keep track of who is definitely coming if you don't have formal replies.

Another alternative is creating your own app. This may sound tricky but there are loads of websites that will guide you through the process, and there's also an option to provide links to the places you have your gift list.

Or if you're really tech savvy, why not build your own website? Once again you can include links to your gift list, have a facility for people to accept or decline invites, and include vital hotel and travel information.

Kara says that while Facebook was helpful in getting the word out about their wedding, she wouldn't ever rely on it if she were organising something formal. 'The thing is, these days people can easily just do a blanket message on Facebook and invite everyone but I really like a formal invite because you know where you are with them. Also, I keep things like that because they mean a lot. I know I'm going to sound like a snob but I have been to weddings where people have done their own invites and some have looked brilliant and others haven't looked that great. I do think it's important to get a professional to do things because first impressions count. I also think it's really nice if all of your wedding stationery ties together. We had our place cards and thank you cards made by the same friend who did our invites so they all matched nicely.'

Tattoo-gether forever

'Our brilliant wedding day was just the start.'

The couple now have two children – Roman, nine, Kara's son from a previous relationship, and baby Arora, aka Rory. Alex says he feels like the luckiest man alive and is excited about the future. 'We've been so blessed to have one of each and we're such a happy family. I'm really excited about what's to come. Our brilliant wedding day was just the start.'

Highlights from the Show... An Invitation to the Wedding

Sheena and Ritesh – An invite would be nice

Sheena's mum has thrown her daughter a Mehndi night, the Indian equivalent of a hen party. Downstairs, her female friends and family have gathered to prepare Sheena for married life. Up in her bedroom, Sheena is furiously brushing her hair and beginning to question if she'd rather stay single. 'I've not heard anything at all,' she says of the invitation she's been expecting from her husband to be. 'I'm not even sure if we have a wedding date,' she wails, close to losing it. 'What are you doing? You should've let me know by now!' Just then, a concerned partygoer pops her head around the door to remind Sheena that everyone is waiting. Brave move...

Emily and Joe – The romantic ransom note

Why say it with flowers when you can send an anonymous note threatening to harm your cat unless you show up on the big day? For groom, Joe, that's exactly the prank he had in mind when it came to presenting his fiancée with a novel invitation to their wedding. Enrolling his mate to don a balaclava, Joe directs the black-clad goon to Emily's house while bravely hiding out of sight. With the note shoved in Emily's face, before the pair scarper, the shocked recipient takes a moment to work out what just happened. 'I feel physically stunned,' she says. 'That was horrible.' Bless!

Victoria and Lloyd – Pack your bags

After nearly three weeks of being kept in the dark while fiancé Lloyd plans their wedding, Victoria starts to feel the strain. 'Everyone is being so secretive,' she says, consoling herself with a glass of wine in the garden. 'I've just had enough now.' The perfect moment, then, for Lloyd's dad to wheel in his son's invitation to the wedding – a suitcase with a note inside: *To my beautiful wife to be – can you please pack this?* Victoria responds by dissolving into tears of confusion and despair. Dad waits for the hole to open up underneath him.

Juan and Alice – The transatlantic cold call

Juan and his best man can barely contain their excitement. Standing on a rooftop terrace, the groom makes a video call home to surprise his bride with an announcement. 'The wedding is going to be this Friday, but it's not in England,' he says, before his mate whisks the camera round to take in the New York skyline. Just for good measure, Juan pops back into frame wearing a comedy Statue of Liberty crown. Giving friends and family a few seconds to cheer, he quickly explains that the trip is going to cost them each £500. It's Juan's older sister who is first to break the silence. 'Get stuffed!' she tells him.

Rosie and Nick – The Christmas cracker

If there's one thing Rosie hates, it's the festive season. Brilliantly, Nick decides to make it central to their wedding, and delivers his invitation in the shape of a huge cracker. Rosie pulls it with her sister, Jess, and sighs to herself as the fake white snow inside scatters all over the sofa. Even the scrolled invitation can't lift her spirits. 'By the looks of things, this is Christmas,' she complains, having worked out Nick's intentions for the theme. 'What is my worst thing?' asks Rosie, before having to spell it out. Jess seems surprised. 'I thought it was sweetcorn?' she says.

Rosie & Dave
Enter the Entourage!

A wedding might be focused on just two people, but behind every bride and groom is a whole cast of critical players. Without them, your special day could well crash and burn in the planning stages. We're talking about those closest to you as a couple in the run-up to a marriage. You might well look to them to take the stress out of much of the organisation, from the caterers and the florists through to the venue hire, but these are also the people you turn to for emotional support when times get tough. And nothing comes much tougher than being in charge of preparing for a wedding...

So, with the engagement announced and a date set for the big day, it's time to turn your attention to the supporting roles. Essentially, you both need to be able to count on people who won't let you down. For the groom, his first port of call is the best man. This is the guy he trusts with his life, or least to see him through the whole process in one piece. The bride can look to her bridesmaids, and even pick out one in particular as her chief. In both cases, it's often a close friend or sibling, but there are no hard and fast rules here. Ultimately, you each have to trust your judgement in making your selection and feel sure that they have your best interests at heart.

At the same time, there's no reason to limit yourselves when it comes to building a support network. The build-up to a marriage is a happy time, but also deeply challenging in bringing it all together. It's here that couples find out who they can truly count on. As a result, friendships are often strengthened or tested to the limit.

Rosie and Dave – The high stakes sea roller

Before Rosie came into his life, and swept him off his feet, Dave could be found working in a surf shop on the Devon coast or catching waves just off the shoreline. Even though Rosie didn't share his passion for water, they proved a perfect match, and Dave set out to prove himself to her by trading

'On paper, a marriage on the rugged island of Lundy, just off the coast of Devon, seemed like a dream location...'

in the laid-back day job for a career as an overhead line engineer. It wasn't just this fun-loving social worker that Dave needed to impress, however. Rosie comes from a large, loving and protective family, and so when Dave popped the question he knew that many others around the love-of-his-life would be questioning his prospects. 'Rightly so, they all wanted the best for Rosie,' he says. 'Her sister had got married a few years earlier, which was an amazing day, and I found that pretty daunting. It set the bar high in many ways. At the same time, I figured this was a chance to showcase my commitment.'

For Rosie, it was the way in which her future husband proposed that told her he might have something romantic in mind. 'I was with my family when he just appeared clutching a box of chocolates and a bottle of champagne,' she says. 'Then he went down on bended knee, produced a ring, and I just cried with happiness.'

Safe in the knowledge that Rosie had said yes, Dave found the courage to pursue an ambitious plan for their wedding. On paper, a marriage on the rugged island of Lundy, just off the coast of Devon, seemed like a dream location. In reality, the couple and their friends had narrowly escaped with their lives on a previous trip to the island when their speedboat ran into trouble in rough seas. Fortunately, disaster had been averted when a nearby dive boat came to their rescue, though the experience left Rosie with no desire to head out to sea again.

Well aware that he was taking a risk, not just with his fiancée's nerves but with the elements as well, Dave cast his net wide for help and support – calling on not just one best man, but two.

'Being asked to stand alongside the bride or groom might be considered a great honour, but it demands a special quality of character.'

Your inner circle

For some couples, picking a best man or chief bridesmaid is a simple task. Aside from their other halves, many people can count on one person in their lives who they consider to be close. But it isn't always just a question of turning to a best friend, brother or sister. Being asked to stand alongside the bride or groom might be considered a great honour, but it demands a special quality of character. So what do you look for in appointing your next-in-command, and how can you be sure they'll rise to the challenge?

The job description

The chief bridesmaid is in charge of marshalling the other bridesmaids and flower girls, organising the hen night, as well as acting as consultant on everything from hair and make-up to the bridal dress and various general arrangements. Critically, she needs to be there with a tissue in hand should the pressure prove too much, and keep the bride focused on the fact that it'll all be worth it in the end. You're doing it for love, after all. 'In the run-up to our wedding it felt like normal life had gone on hold,' says Rosie. 'My bridesmaids were there to offer me not just companionship but reassurance, and that meant so much to me.'

As well as staging your stag night, the best man is expected to take good care of the rings and produce them on cue at the ceremony. In addition, he should be on hand to help buy or hire suits, make sure the groom shows up on time (and in good shape) and also help everyone present throughout the day feel comfortable. This only stops when it comes to the speeches, when your best man traditionally sends you up with a sense of fondness and mischief. For Dave, opting for two best men – the memorably named Tonky and Spew – meant he could call upon different qualities and combine them into one role. 'Tonky is always up for a laugh, and Spew can be a great leveller. I needed both personalities at different times throughout the planning. That was critical for me.'

The human qualities

A level head

In the run-up to your marriage – and we're not talking about the dress here – there will be times when you feel the squeeze. Planning a wedding always brings some pressure and stress, and chances are you'll both carry that on your shoulders. So can your best man and chief bridesmaid help you to share that load? Do they work well under a deadline, and keep a level head should you ever feel like yours is spinning around with so much to sort out? For Rosie, having a straight-talking sister in her entourage proved to be an asset when it came to addressing a malfunction in Dave's choice of dresses for the bridesmaids. 'She spoke her mind,' says Rosie, 'but that came from a good place, and as a result things changed for the better.'

Organisational flair

Attention grooms! You could be asking a man to multi-task here. This might well narrow the field of candidates, but it's vital that your choice is aware of the things-to-do list ahead. Much is down to you, of course, in terms of the role you'd like your best man to play. At the very least, he'll be expected to organise a stag night, and take care of the rings before the ceremony, but realistically he'll be at your side every step of the way. On the day, the best man often takes the role of host. He's there to welcome guests and make them feel comfortable, and serves as the go-to-guy for fixing unforeseen events. All with a confident smile on his face. The chief bridesmaid is likely to be equally busy, tasked as she is with taking care of the bridesmaids. So, if

you've opted to go young here, be sure she's comfortable working with children. As Rosie had chosen friends and family as bridesmaids that she knew would all get on, her entourage proved low maintenance. 'We've known each other for ages,' she says, 'and that made life easier for us all.'

People Skills

If your closest friend or sibling also happens to be painfully shy, you might want to reflect on whether they can deliver the goods as your next-in-command. The role of best man and chief bridesmaid demands a level of sociability and charisma. You're the stars, but they're the supporting act. 'Spew and Tonky did an amazing job on the day,' says Dave. 'Just making sure the guests got across from the mainland in one piece was a massive effort.'

A Sense of Humour

Your best man and chief bridesmaid are there to see you through the highs and lows of the build-up to your wedding. If they can laugh in the face of adversity, you're half way there. For a groom who encountered setback after setback in a bid to get his ambitious plans off the ground, good humour seemed to be the only thing holding back Dave's tears. 'I spent eight lonely, windswept days on Lundy to qualify as a resident, so we could officially marry on the island, only to discover that the bride needed to be informed in advance. As that was out of the question, I had to book a registry office in Devon. We could still have a blessing and reception on Lundy, but my stay turned out to be a complete waste of time. When Tonky and Spew found out, they just cracked up. I couldn't help laughing with them, which worked as a pressure release so I could focus on my next steps.'

When a wedding plan comes together...

'What I needed from my best men just then was emotional support, and they delivered it.'

Approaching the eve of his wedding, Dave knew that his plans could still sink. With boat crossings at the mercy of the weather, he'd effectively gambled on a factor that was out of his control. 'It was really stressful,' he reflects. 'At that moment, I had done everything to prepare for the wedding. There was nothing more that I could do but wait and see what the wind was like in the morning.' Exhausted from his efforts in getting everything

ready for the big day, Dave found himself facing a long and nerve-wracking night. 'What I needed from my best men just then was emotional support, and they delivered it,' he continues. 'More than anything else, if it had all gone wrong I needed to know they would back me up in the decisions I had taken. I guess I had chosen them because I could count on them to stand by me. Without a doubt, they stopped me from feeling alone and kept me strong, even when the wedding day dawned with bright blue skies!'

For a groom with a high stakes plan, Dave's wedding to Rosie proved picture perfect. With a church blessing and reception, followed by a boat cruise back to the mainland for the wedding party and guests, the couple look back with nothing but gratitude towards their entourage for helping to make it happen. But what advice do they have for anyone in the process of appointing a best man and bridesmaids? In Dave's view, the key is in turning to someone you can rely on even if they think your ideas are crazy! 'You just need to be sure that they'll give one hundred percent when it comes to making everything go as smoothly as possible,' he says. 'I needed people prepared to run with my plans without question. In a way, even when things looked bleak, that gave me the courage to believe that I could still pull it off.' As for Rosie, it's quite clear in her mind that without the support of their entourage the whole process of planning a wedding would've fallen apart. 'The stress levels can really start to climb,' she says, 'which is why you need that calming presence from the people you want around you.'

Highlights from the Show… Enter the Entourage!

Ryan and Fern – the fine bromance

The best man's role is to support the groom in the run-up to his wedding. When Fern leaves her fiancé, Ryan, so he can plan their happy day, best man Matt shows up and literally takes her place. 'They're like kids together,' she complains, as the boys move into the couple's caravan and the bromance blossoms. From trying out wedding dresses on Fern's behalf to securing their friendship forever on the stag night with matching buttock tattoos, the pair prove inseparable. 'He even took my bed,' grumbles Fern, having finally reclaimed Ryan as her husband. 'I'm never moving out again!'

David and Eve – Six unhappy bridesmaids

David had high hopes for the 1950s-style pink and plum coloured dresses he'd picked out for Eve's bridesmaids. Inviting them round for a big reveal, he escorts them upstairs and ushers them into a bedroom so they can check out his choices. But even before making it back down to the ground floor to await their response, David's confidence deserts him. It leaves him waiting nervously on the sofa with his mum and best man. 'They're laughing,' mum observed optimistically. 'Yeah, at them,' David mutters, as he finally emerges from denial to recognise that each and every dress is dramatically wrong in size.

Rena and Wesley – Don't mess with mum

So, Rena's bridesmaids have assembled to see their dresses for the first time. You just know that faces are going to fall before heads start wobbling. 'I can't wear this!' declares one, waggling her index finger back and forth. 'Ain't happenin... ain't happenin... THIS AIN'T HAPPENIN!' Moments later, Wesley's mum arrives to check out the dresses for herself. A practical lady, well aware that time is against them and the bride is eggshell-delicate, she encourages the girls to review their opinion. The result? After much pursing of lips, Wesley's choice of bridesmaids' dresses very much *is* happening.

Nicole and Sean – A vision shared

Harry Potter-nut, Sean, has brought his best man, Liam, to tour his first choice of venue. The pair stand before a grand, imposing castle, with manicured grounds where Sean can see games of 'Quidditch' taking place in his mind's eye. 'It's exactly what I want,' he says admiringly, and looks to Liam for the kind of support and approval that every groom needs when tasked with planning his own wedding. With his hands in his pockets, Liam assesses the vaulted windows and the turrets. 'It's shit,' he says simply.

Mike and Katie – You had one job!

'The proposal was a bit of a disaster,' reveals Katie. 'He just dumped himself on a sofa next to me, threw this ring at me and says "are you going to marry me, then?"'. Starting low but aiming high, Mike puts his heart and soul into creating a show-stopping wedding for his bride. Everything goes to plan until the groom and his best man, Ross, set off for the ceremony. 'Did you pick the rings up?' asks Mike, to which Ross responds with a look sure to leave every groom stone cold. Cue a mad dash to collect the missing items, and happy smiles from the bride who has no idea what her new husband just went through.

Jay & Ian

A Dress to Die ~~in~~ for

Ask any bride to name the most important aspect of her wedding, chances are she'll go for the dress. It's the one thing that has to be exactly right. Even with just a single stitch out of place, or a missing sequin, there's a good chance you'll see tears on the day – and not in a good way.

So, why is choosing a dress such a big deal? What is it about something you'll only wear only once that means so much? For many brides, this is the moment they used to dream about as little girls. Quite literally, it's a chance to be a fairy tale princess just for one day, and celebrate their union in style. The choice, style and even colour of dress may differ according to religion, culture or taste, but ultimately every bride wants to look and feel beautiful. The groom may have no idea how much effort goes into achieving this, or what's at stake with expectation set so high, but it all comes down to the woman of their dreams stepping up the aisle in something that dazzles, enchants and inspires.

But where do you start when it comes to choosing the ultimate dress? Do you go traditional or original, strapless, sleeveless, A-line or Empire, beaded, lace or satin? With so many styles and designs on offer, how can you be sure you're making the right decision, and who can you trust to support you – or even tailor it for that matter? The process can be fun, adventurous and also deeply stressful, so how do you manage those expectations, and deal with any disappointments? With so many different factors in the mix, the dress can come to represent both the highs and lows of the planning process. You could climb into one that feels perfect, and sets you up with giddy excitement for the day, only for the slightest rip to tear into your dreams and bring it all crashing down.

So, with the wisdom of hindsight from a groom who went half-way around the world for his bride's dress, let's look at how to take the strain out of the seams as much as the selection process.

Ian and Jay – The long-distance wedding dress

Ask part-time model, Jay, about her hopes for the dress she would wear on her wedding day, and she'll take you back to her teenage years. 'I spent a lot of time thinking about it,' she says. 'Together with my friends, we'd talk about what we'd wear if we ever got married, and that never really stopped. It's been like a lifelong thing! To begin, I was into the whole idea of a big dress, but as I grew up my tastes became more simple and relaxed.'

In theory, meeting Jay's wedding dress needs should've been straightforward for fiancé, Ian. As this chipper fleet manager discovered, however, choosing the right one is fraught with difficulties he just hadn't anticipated. 'It all started with me not actually knowing what kind of dress she had in mind,' he says. 'It meant I was faced with a blank page.' For some grooms, but not many, this might've been an opportunity for

'Without a doubt, being efficient can pay off when it comes to planning your wedding... unless, of course, you decide to stage a stag night in Bangkok in the hope of picking up the wedding dress while you're out there...'

creativity and invention. For Ian, it proved to be the beginning of a test of courage and conviction that threatened to undermine their big day.

A picture perfect couple from Stockport, Jay and Ian first met on a night out on the town. As the designated driver for her friends that evening, and stone cold sober, Jay's first impression of her future husband might well have given her a hint of how he'd plan their wedding. 'He was quite a Jack-the-lad,' she laughs. 'He approached me with this cheeky smile and a chat up line.' Understandably, winging it in this way didn't bring an immediate return for Ian, though he freely confesses to maturing in the years that passed before they finally got together. By the time he felt the time had arrived to propose, Jay found herself facing a man in full-on romantic mode. 'Ian took me out for a dinner at my favourite pub,' she remembers. 'While we were out, he'd arranged for my flatmates to light hundreds of candles for my return. So, I walked into this amazing surprise, and found a card on the table addressed to "my fiancée." Then he got down on one knee, and naturally I said "yes!"'

With the wedding date set, and Ian in sole charge of the planning, Jay figured that Ian would build on such a well-prepared approach. Sure enough, Ian embraced the process with confidence and high hopes, only to make one judgement that he looks back on now with a grimace. 'I looked at what I had to do as if it was a jigsaw. Unfortunately, I didn't stop to think that the wedding dress is more than just another piece. It's the centrepiece.

Without getting that into place first, nothing else fits.'

Without a doubt, being efficient can pay off when it comes to planning your wedding. Combining tasks is a sure-fire way to tick them off the list that little bit quicker. Unless, of course, you decide to stage a stag night in Bangkok in the hope of picking up the wedding dress while you're out there. For Ian, who figured he could purchase a quality dress at a fraction of UK prices, it seemed like a smart and money-wise move. So, with the boys in tow, he set off to make the dress selection look like a walk in the park. What could go wrong?

Dress decisions

So, what goes into picking out the dress you could've been born to wear? It's not rocket science, but close in terms of the complexity of questions you need to address. Here's our at-a-glance guide to the main considerations…

What Kind of Wedding?

Whether you're getting married in a church, registry office or civil ceremony, the nature of the occasion is sure to inform your choice of dress. If you're unsure of any formalities, have a chat with the individual conducting the marriage first. It's better to do your homework here, rather than take a gamble and feel out of place on your big day.

What About You?

We're talking about a dress that's all about the bride. Every stitch has to be enriched with your personality. First and foremost, this means you need to feel completely comfortable wearing it. Of course, it's easy

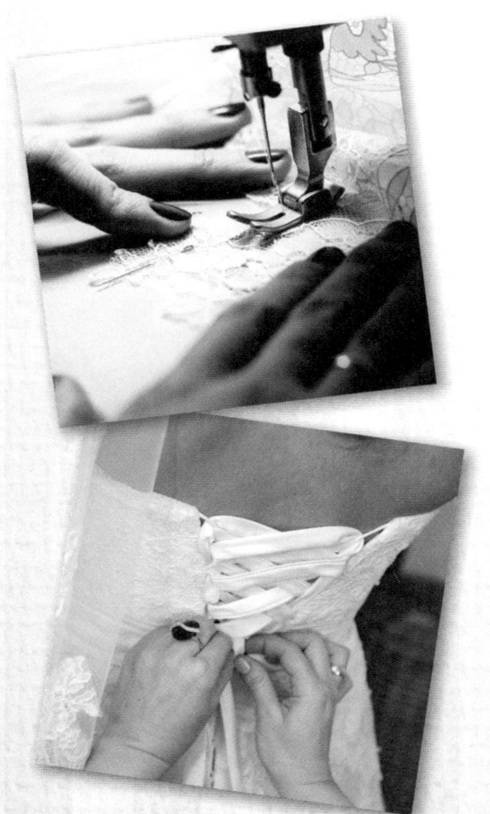

to feel tempted into something that looks striking but doesn't feel like a second skin. You just need to ask what's guaranteed to help you bring out a heartfelt smile on your big day. Also think about your bridesmaids here. It shouldn't dictate what dress you buy, but look at the choices on offer and ask how best their outfits would complement the look.

Where To Shop?

Catering for all budgets, it's possible to pick out your dream dress from a high-street rail – so don't be quick to discount all possibilities. Allow yourself plenty of time to shop around, from bridal shops to department stores. Also factor in time for fittings, while consulting wedding guides, magazines and websites in search of inspiration. Even if money is tight, it's worth considering a dressmaker to see what's on offer. You might also want to seek out a seamstress who can make alterations to an off-the-peg dress so it feels tailor-made for you.

Who's Helping?

Like any shopping expedition, it's always good to have a second opinion. On this occasion, in selecting a wedding dress, you need someone who knows you inside out, and whose judgement you trust. From your mum to the chief bridesmaid, be sure to choose wisely and feel confident that they'll respect your feelings. Would you prefer one opinion you truly value or a group appraisal from a bunch of mates? The choice is yours, of course, which makes selecting your dress such a challenge. The key is to approach it in a way that makes you feel like you've considered all the options and made a decision that feels just right.

That dress

'Girls spend years thinking about their dream dress. I had a week and a half.'

After a 6,000 mile-long shopping trip for Jay's dress, and with £1,600 spent on flights to Thailand, Ian made a series of discoveries that caused his heart to quicken. 'All the dresses were made with Thai women in mind,' he says. 'They also used different size measurements, and the cost wasn't much different than it would've been back home. On top of all that, I still didn't know what I should be looking for. Girls spend years thinking about their dream dress. I had a week and a half. In the end, after thirteen hours of trawling a strip of shops dedicated to bridal gowns, I just caved. Basically, I picked out one that caught my eye, which was fairly simple with nice embroidery, and then bartered as best I could so I could pay for it.'

Back home, Jay's sole concern was that Ian would pick out a big princess-style dress. 'I thought he might compensate for the lad he used to be when we first met,' she says. 'He'd matured, and wanted to treat me like a princess. I felt that he'd express it by going for something big and showy, even though that isn't me at all.' As it turned out, the style of wedding dress was the least of Jay's worries. On setting eyes on Ian's choice, which frankly hadn't travelled well, her reaction switched from high excitement to disappointment to dismay. 'At first I was impressed by the vintage style, and the fact that it was detailed,' she says. 'Then I started looking more closely, and realised it was mucky, and that a lot of the gems embroidered into it had fallen off. It was basically a broken dress that didn't even fit me, and I just cried.'

Saving the day

'From experience, it's totally down to the bride, and how she feels in it. Even her mother couldn't pick one out for her.'

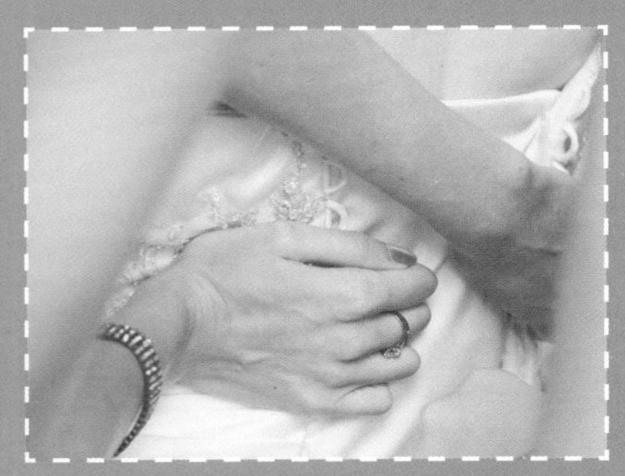

Having worked out that a wedding dress is more than just another jigsaw piece in the wedding planner's puzzle, and with just 24 hours to go before the ceremony, Ian reacted like any groom in the same situation. 'I panicked,' he says simply. 'I also knew it had to be sorted out, and just headed for the nearest bridal shop. Fortunately, I really liked the first one I saw. But what mattered to me most was that I knew it was the right size.'

As dress rescues go, Ian's swift actions saved his wedding day. 'The second one wasn't something I'd have chosen,' admits Jay, 'but because it felt better when I wore it, I felt better. Then, on the day, with my hair and make-up done, I actually felt amazing in it.'

So, in Jay's experience, the fit proved to be the factor that helped her to enjoy a wedding staged at an old-time theatre. But in handing down advice to brides set to follow in her footsteps, what else can she offer to help them make the right choice? 'It was all about how I felt in it,' she says. 'Had Ian's first choice actually been the right size, I might've felt more relaxed about the finish. Missing gems or little tears can be repaired, and that might be an issue if you're thinking of a vintage or second-hand dress, but at the end of the day it had to be something that felt really comfortable.'

Understandably, despite snatching a dream wedding from the jaws of defeat, Ian is certain that his dress-buying days are behind him. 'There's no way I would ever want to be involved in buying something so serious,' he declares. 'From experience, it's totally down to the bride, and how she feels in it. Even her mother couldn't pick one out for her.'

Such was the stress behind the process that newly-wed Ian found himself in tears at the reception. 'It was just sheer relief at seeing her look so beautiful after everything I had been through.' As for Jay, her husband's efforts didn't go unappreciated. 'He put his heart into it,' she said. 'Despite all the grief with the dress, Ian did all he could to give me the perfect day, and that's something I will never forget.'

Highlights from the Show...
A Dress to Die ~~in~~ for

Pippa and Tony – The wedding dress recovery

Tony has high hopes that he's found the perfect dress for fiancée, Pippa. His choice certainly looks like a million dollars when the boutique assistant presents it, but what matters is how it makes the bride feel. Stepping out from the changing room, one look at Pippa's crumpling face is enough to know that all is not well. Despite her mother's assurances that she looks just fine, the bride's tears start to flow. It's not just the colour, she says. It's the buttons... and the hips. Fortunately, Tony turns it around with a replacement dress that brings her out in smiles.

Sheena and Ritesh – The chicken fillet fix

Leaving Ritesh, her comedy-gold groom to plan the wedding, 'Ricky-style', Sheena is braced for anything. But even she struggles to keep smiling when her bridal dress turns out to be a size too big in all the wrong places. A member of Sheena's entourage calls Ricky to break the news. Rather than offer to sort out a replacement immediately, Ricky thinks outside the box (and arguably outside of his mind). 'Take her to McDonalds,' he suggests. 'Fill her out a bit.' 'I don't think her boobs will grow with a Maccy D's!' comes the diplomatic response, which is when our groom ditches the eating plan in favour of a sensible solution.

Ian and Reanna – The groom done good

Together for seven years before marriage beckons, Reanna can only hope that Ian knows her better than anyone. But leaving him to organise a big fat Greek wedding, and with her family to keep sweet, the bride's confidence begins to thin. Come the day of the dress reveal, Reanna is braced for anything. Ian's choice is the last thing she imagined, featuring the low-cut neckline and big skirt she hoped he would avoid… and she loves it! 'He's the fashionista!' gasps the bride on trying it on. 'It's glamorous. So romantic!'

Ben and Sarah – The groom could've done better

'I just don't want to look fat on my wedding day,' says Sarah demurely, on a trip out to see Ben's choice of dress. 'It better look friggin' decent!'. That she bursts into the wrong kind of tears before stepping into the bridal boutique is perhaps a sign that things are set to go badly wrong. Sure enough, when presented with a big dress she wouldn't be seen dead in, Sarah crumples. Mum is on hand to coax her weeping daughter into the changing room. Duly, Sarah closes the curtain behind her as if she might not survive the ordeal.

Scott and Verity – the eBay bridal dress

In a moment of genius, or madness depending on how you look at it, rock-star-turned-zoo-keeper, Scott, looks online for his bride's wedding dress. Skipping the boutique websites, he heads straight for eBay in search of a bargain. Why pay £1,500 when you can have one shipped from abroad for less than £100? As Verity discovers, wiping away tears as she picks at the loose beads and threads, there's often a good reason. At a price worth paying, a seamstress saves the day, and possibly Scott's marriage – transforming Verity's wedding dress and turning her frown upside down.

Harry & Mel
Let's Accessorise!

Ask anyone what goes into making a wedding and they'll pick out the popular features. From the ceremony to the reception, the dress, the disco and the dancing, it's easy to put together the basic building blocks for the day. But in focusing on the big picture it's also easy to forget the details. We could be talking about anything from a clever use of drapes to candle holders and cake stands. As well as accessorising your wedding, it's important to consider the finishing touches for the main players, from buttonholes for the boys, bouquets for the bridesmaids to a striking pair of shoes that showcases the bridal dress to the best effect. As any couple who have tied the knot will tell you, it's the little things that can make all the difference.

So at such a busy time, with so many pressing things to tick off the checklist, how can you be sure that nothing is overlooked?

In planning your wedding, it's always good to have a keen eye when looking for inspiration. Something minor might well come to your attention that you hadn't previously considered, such as confetti that complements the colour scheme for your day. With tailoring to make things feel personal, that little something could just be what everyone talks about for a long time to come.

Accessorising your wedding can also bring out your creative side. Even if you're planning a traditional day, here's a chance to add style and flair in an understated but memorable way. It may not be much, but it could well say more about your personality than anything else, as one *Don't Tell The Bride* couple – and a pair of yellow wellies – demonstrated with such panache.

Harry and Mel – catch of the day

'He proposed with a Haribo ring...'

Harry is a man of the sea. A fisherman from the beautiful seaside village of Manorbier in Wales, he's more likely to be found on his boat than dry land. 'I just love the nice views, the birds and the dolphins,' he says of his love of the ocean life, 'while catching mad stuff like crabs or whelks.' His fiancée, Mel, is a mobile hairdresser. She's passionate about Harry, but not so wild when he returns from a day at the offshore office. 'Harry is really good looking and fit, with nice curly hair and muscles,' she says, 'but I don't like the smell of fish. Or whelks. Or fish guts. So, when Harry comes home I normally say, "can you strip off at the front door? You stink!"'

Despite not sharing Harry's love of the high seas, Mel is clearly in deep with her man, and overjoyed when he popped the question – quite literally in the sweetest way possible. 'He proposed with a Haribo ring,' she laughs. 'I wore it for about ten minutes before it got a little bit sticky. Then all the rest of the sweets went, so I ate the ring!' Not only did this charming, simple and inventive gesture sum up Harry's personality, it would prove a taster of his approach to planning the wedding that followed. 'Harry has always been very thoughtful,' says Mel. 'He might like going out drinking with his mates and stuff, but there's so much more to him than that.'

With such high praise from Mel, it would be easy to think that Harry sailed through the planning and preparation of their wedding without a hitch. In truth, rather than call upon an in-built instinct for creating what would be a perfect day for his bride, Harry's first port of call was the internet. 'It's a brilliant source of inspiration,' he says. 'I was looking through loads of pictures, working out what I liked and didn't like, and that helped me to shape my own ideas.'

Even with Mel's feelings about the sea in mind, Harry felt sure that a nautical theme would be the perfect way to launch their lives as man and wife. With plans for a ceremony overlooking the beach, followed by a fishing boat trip to a harbour-side reception, he knew he'd have his work cut out to impress his bride. 'If I was going to win her over then absolutely everything had to look really nice,' he says, which is when our groom turned his attention to the accessories that could make or break their big day.

Small things, big impact

'Every couple has different tastes, of course, so the little touches that can mean so much are entirely down to you.'

In shaping your wedding, it's vital that you cover every aspect of the planning process. It's natural to focus on the main elements, of course, and so everything from the venues to the dress are bound to take priority. But even the most striking location for your ceremony or reception has to feel special to you, and that requires some imagination. Start to think on this level, and it's easy to see how your 'to do' list can lengthen. Accessorising your wedding is an effective way to personalise the day. The catch is we could be talking about anything from the choice of font for your invitations upwards.

Every couple has different tastes, of course, so the little touches that can mean so much are entirely down to you. In setting up the best day for his bride, and with his research complete, Harry prioritised his planning to make sure that time for the final brushstrokes didn't run out on him. 'Once I'd dealt with the big stuff, which involved booking a longhouse for the ceremony, sorting out the reception, the dress and the transport, I started thinking about ways to make it feel special to Mel,' he says. 'The fact is you can't really focus on the details without first sorting out your basic wedding. Once that's ticked off, the ideas start to flow and you can begin to work out what extras are really going to work well.'

A little list

So, when it comes to those minor aspects of your day, what are the major considerations? Here are five features of an unforgettable wedding that may not be uppermost in your mind:

The Hair

It might be something that you know how to handle on a regular basis, but if you're aiming for a special style on the day, be sure to give yourself time to experiment. Consult your hairdresser in advance, or a stylist you trust. Together, work on a look that helps you to feel comfortable and relaxed, and brings out the best in your dress.

The Make-Up

Practice really does make perfect here, so create every opportunity to establish what works best for you. Consult friends you trust, visit beauty counters together or even consider hiring a professional make-up artist to take away the strain on your big day. Also, think about your nails. From trying out different colours, opting for a quality polish or visiting a nail bar on the eve of your big day, these little touches could just complete your look.

The Name Cards

This might not seem like a big deal, but without them you could be looking at a reception packed with confused guests who have no idea where they should be sitting. Name cards can be ordered in advance, and it's worth having a wedding directory to hand for any suppliers you need. Alternatively, you could opt to write them yourself, or create a stamp and print each one personally. This might take more time and planning, but it's a sure-fire way to charm your guests.

The Guest Book

A wedding day can often pass in a blur for the bride and groom. At such an exciting moment in your lives, and with so many close friends and family around you, it can be hard to spend quality time with everyone present. A guest book allows people to write down special messages for the couple, or thoughts and reflections about the day. Not only can it form an everlasting record of the day, it can be a fun and inviting way to bring your guests closer together. With the right touch – and a careful choice of writing instrument and tome – a guest book can become a talking point at your wedding. It can also be something everyone has a hand in creating.

The Personal Touch

When it comes to investing your personality in the wedding, don't be afraid to unleash your inventive side. Quite simply, you can accessorise pretty much any aspect of the day and make it feel as if it belongs to you. And if you're lacking the confidence to do a good job here, be ready to reach out for support, as Harry discovered when it came to bringing a taste of life on the ocean waves to his wedding...

Get creative, and collaborate!

'Then I started thinking how that whole aquatic theme could work into the wedding. With the bouquets and flowers, for example, I realised I could do something special simply by adding shells, netting and starfish.'

'It all started with the yellow wellies,' says Harry. 'That's what fishermen wear, and I'm known for wearing a pair everywhere I go. So, right from the start I knew I wanted to get married in them. I also figured Mel would look great in a pair instead of normal bridal shoes! Then I started thinking how that whole aquatic theme could work into the wedding. With the bouquets and flowers, for example, I realised I could do something special simply by adding shells, netting and starfish. The trouble is,' he confesses, 'I didn't know where to start.' Instead of ditching the concept, Harry found a florist he liked who was prepared to work with his idea. 'We chose simple yellow flowers to match the wellies, and she took it from there,' he says. 'The results were amazing and admired by everyone.'

For Mel, the arrival of the bouquets on the morning of their wedding served to calm any misgivings she had about Harry's plans. 'I was so impressed as soon as I saw the shells in amongst the flowers. They were really pretty, and very artistic.' It wasn't until later, however, having arrived at the reception in her bridal wellies, that Mel appreciated the extent of Harry's finishing touches. 'The whole place was decorated in fishing gear,' she says. 'There were arrangements with anchors, sand, paddles and buoys, the kind of stuff that normally stinks, but it had all been scrubbed up and looked amazing. If anything, I was shocked that Harry and his mates had done such a good job with so little.'

Bringing it all together

For a groom who had gone online for inspiration, Harry's efforts to personalise his wedding to Mel clearly came from the heart, and proved both memorable and unique. What's more, with access to all the fishing equipment, and after strenuous cleaning efforts, his finishing touches didn't put a serious dent in the budget. 'It brought out my feminine side!' he laughs. 'To an extent it all fell together, but I couldn't have done it without help from friends and people who could lend their expertise.' As for learning from the experience, Harry's advice when it comes to accessorising a wedding is to dig deep into the power of the imagination. 'It's your day,' he says simply. 'Ask yourself what you'd like to see in the details and make it happen. Even if you need help, there's no need to settle for second best.'

Without doubt, Harry's triumph in topping off the wedding with such a creative and considerate eye proved to be a happy surprise for his bride. 'It taught me something about him that I'll never forget,' says Mel. 'Not only is he really thoughtful, he's quite capable of doing stuff that I normally take care of myself. Ever since our wedding, whenever the house needs to look at its best, I don't take any excuses off him! I know Harry can make things look beautiful when he puts his mind to the job, and I only have to look back at our big day to be reminded of it.'

If fisherman Harry's triumph in accessorising the wedding wasn't enough, he's since turned his attention to creating additions for the home. Together with Mel, he's now the proud parent of two little minnows in the form of daughters, Honey and Tilly. Congratulations, guys!

Highlights from the Show... Let's Accessorise!

Hannah and Andy – The wrong shoes

At any wedding, it's a brave man who elects to choose the shoes for his bride. For all his efforts, the groom might as well pick them out blindfolded, as demonstrated by Hannah and her bridesmaids when they unbox Andy's choice and take turns in pouring scorn. 'They look like something your nan wears,' sniffs Hannah before clocking the cheap price tag. While her friends continue to fall about laughing, our bride flops on a chair with a shoe in hand, before hurling it across the fitting room floor. So, that's a 'no', then.

Kallie and Grantt – The steam punk accessories

Bride Kallie is inspired by 50's glamour, and while Grantt loves the retro look he's also keen to throw in something a little more... futuristic. Rather than tour the bridal dress stores, Grantt makes himself comfortable on the carpet at home and breaks out the notepad and pens. 'I've had lots and lots of ideas,' he says, having drawn up some sketches. 'Probably the most interesting is my steam punk wedding dress,' he adds, and proudly holds up a picture of what looks like a bride being consumed from behind by a gigantic spider. As accessories go it's unique, but possibly not in keeping with the day, as Grantt wisely realises for himself. 'She'd kill me,' he says, laughing like a man who has just dodged a bullet.

Levi and Jade – The bridal boots

'I'm only five foot one,' says Jade, out scouting for the ideal shoes to go with her dream dress, 'so I'll need some heels.' Across town, at Stoke City's football pitch where Jade's surprise wedding is set to take place, Levi and his best man, Damo, sagely consider health and safety issues. 'If there's water on the pitch it can get quite slippery,' warns club representative, Rob. 'I think football boots for the bride, to be fair.' Later that day, Levi and Damo find Jade the perfect pair – complete with stripes and studs – and a bargain at fifteen quid. Back of the net, boys!

Nathan and Nikki – The trim is in

As every groom knows, if you're going to choose an 18th-century Napoleonic uniform for your big day then you'll be naked without the accessories. For Nathan, it's the show-stopping shoulder sash that completes the look. It sweeps across his brocaded chest, which he puffs proudly on appraising himself in front of the dressing room mirror. 'You look like a bit of a knob,' his brother offers harshly, but it falls on deaf ears. Feeling like a million ransacked gold coins, Nathan is ready to advance the bridal campaign.

David and Lucy – The lingerie spree

'I'm after a bra to go under the bridal gown,' mumbles David to the sales assistant, barely able to look her in the eye. 'And some... things,' he adds, while gesturing at his midriff. It's a blessing that the assistant has seen grooms like this before, and knows David isn't talking about some nice silky underwear for himself. Even so, the price tag comes as a shock, as well as an excuse for David to step outside to confer with his best man. 'This is a lone ranger operation,' he decides eventually, as if lives are at stake here, before heading back in to seal the deal.

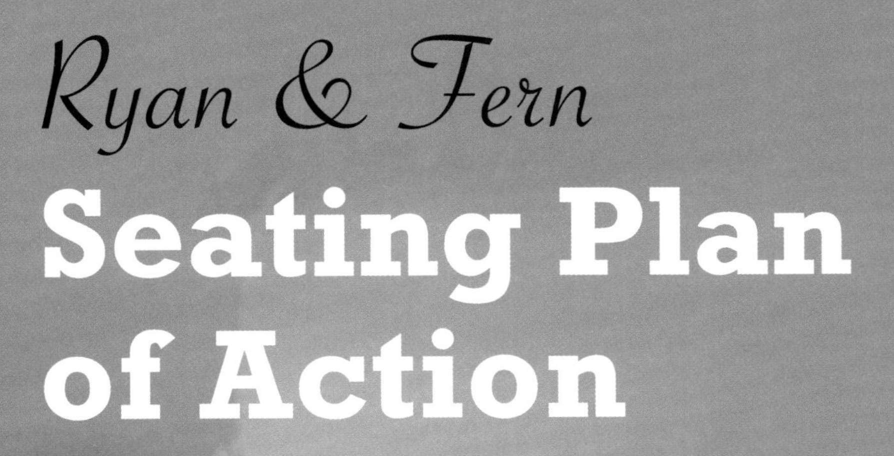

Ryan & Fern
Seating Plan of Action

Let's face it; the two most important people at a wedding are always going to be the bride and groom. But it's the friends and family who make it even more special and help make the day go with a bang. Whether you're having an invite-everyone extravaganza or a small, intimate affair, the guest list is key. Do you sacrifice one of your close mates so you can invite Auntie Ethel who you last saw when you were five? Or do you ditch the extended family and make it all about your mates?

The size of the bash is always a key factor in what kind of wedding reception you're going to have, so it's all about making a firm decision and sticking to it. The guest list can be tricky because you don't want to offend people by not inviting them, but equally you don't want to overstretch yourself and invite people out of duty. The bottom line is that a party is nothing without people, so it's time to play the numbers game.

Ryan and Fern – teenage dream

'I was addicted to *Don't Tell The Bride* and I applied on a whim. I was never going to be a bridezilla type, I just wanted to be married, so I didn't mind handing over the responsibility to Ryan one little bit.'

By Fern's own admission, hers and Ryan's courtship wasn't all hearts, flowers and lavish dinners. When they met she was just 17 and working in Next, while joiner Ryan was a youthful 19. Their early dating days involved a lot of texting and, erm, pretending not to be interested in each other. 'There's really nothing terribly romantic about how we got together,' Fern begins honestly. 'We're both from the Lancashire area and one night we ended up at the same party. We exchanged numbers and it went from there. We were both so young we didn't do proper dating or anything; we just started texting and meeting up more often. I tried to play it cool but I knew I felt strongly for Ryan and I knew I wanted to tame him. Deep down I think we both knew we were falling in love with each other from quite early on.'

The couple, who are now proud parents to Seth, four, (who was conceived on their wedding night!) and Nancy, one, were together for four years before Ryan got down on one knee. 'My parents threw me a 21st birthday party at a bistro in town and Ryan proposed to me there in front of everybody. I knew it was coming at some point because I'd picked out a ring the previous year. But because I'd chosen a right whopper he was paying it off in stages and I had no idea how long that would take. I really loved the fact all of my friends and family were there for the big moment and there was no way I was saying no. Not with that ring!'

Ryan always planned on having an element of surprise to the proposal, but he was also keen to make sure everyone got a good look at Fern's pricey sparkler. 'I wanted to propose when Fern wasn't expecting it and, because I like to make a show of things, I wanted everyone to see me do it. I'd spent a lot of money on the ring so it was important to show it off. I'd known for a long time she was the one for me so it was always just a matter of time before I got down on one knee.'

With the ring firmly on her finger, it was time to start planning the wedding. And it was Fern who came up with the idea of involving *Don't Tell The Bride*. 'I was addicted to the show and I applied on a whim. I was never going to be a bridezilla type, I just wanted to be married, so I didn't mind handing over the responsibility to Ryan one little bit.'

And it sounds like she made the right decision. 'I have to say, my time on *Don't Tell The Bride* ended up being some of the best three weeks of my life,' admits Ryan. 'I love organising things and being the centre of attention so it was perfect for me. My only headache was the guest list…'

Be my guest

'I wanted a massive wedding with everyone I knew there, but I also wanted a nice location so I had to compromise.'

The guest list is all about prioritising. Are plus-ones necessary? Can you afford to extend the invitation to people you don't have any kind of emotional attachment to? Or is money no object and who cares if you don't recognise half of the people there? It's important not to invite people just because you feel like you should. Ask yourself some important questions: Have you spoken to that person in the last year? Will you still be in touch in five years time? Are you asking them out of guilt or duty?

Another thing you have to take into account is the size of the venue. A building can only hold so many people so check how many you can accommodate before you start inviting people (if you want the perfect excuse to invite less people, simply book a smaller place).

If you want a big bash, an outside do may seem more appealing. But remember that if it rains those people have still got to shelter somewhere, so you need a large room on standby.

Showman Ryan wanted to his wedding to be large and lavish, but he had to rein things in when he found his ideal venue. 'At first it felt like I'd done things the wrong way round because the place I chose, Oulton Hall near Leeds, could only hold 100 guests. Obviously once I'd put down the deposit I had to stick to that number so I did panic a bit initially. But actually it worked out well because I had to be ruthless. I wanted a massive wedding with everyone I knew there, but I also wanted a nice location so I had to compromise. It was impossible to have all the people I wanted. Fern's mum, Shelly, gave me a list of people I should invite from her side, but in the end I couldn't invite everyone on it due to space.'

Fern was very happy she got to stay out of the decision-making when it came to the attendees, especially as she would have found it hard to make a call on who was and wasn't invited. 'We've got a lot of mutual friends and Ryan could have gone on and on and on with the guest list. I didn't want him to upset anyone but there was a budget so he had to have a cut-off point. Ryan and I had chatted about who we would invite to our wedding long before we did *Don't Tell The Bride* and there were a few people I immediately said not to worry about, in the nicest possible way. They were mainly old school friends I hadn't seen for years. I didn't have much of a chance to think about numbers but in my opinion there could never have been too many people there. And, if I'm being honest, I would have been disappointed if there had been too few people there.'

In the end, Fern feels like Ryan got the balance just right. 'The most important thing is being surrounded by your friends and family and having a really nice time. If it had been a small service I would have been shocked more than anything. Ryan is a proper show-off so I knew he would have wanted a lot of people around him, I had the bridesmaids I wanted, which was my main priority, so when it came to the people it was just about perfect for me. And of course I got to escape all the stress of it.'

It's always nice to give guests as much warning as possible so they can organise their outfits/travel/accommodation, especially if they're making the trip from far away. So maybe don't take a leaf out of Ryan's book and have invites languishing in your van two days before the event. 'One of the invites I forgot to post was for Fern's nana. So one of her nana's had been sent her invitation and the other one hadn't, which was very bad form. Luckily everyone already knew they were invited because I'd told them; in the end I phoned the people I was worried about. Don't tell Fern but I think there are still a few invites lying around in my van to this day.'

Who, what, when?

The bride and groom often want to invite people to different parts of the day. Of course, you want your nearest and dearest to be at the ceremony and wedding breakfast, and the reception/evening do is the ideal place to invite people you're not as close to.

Your guest list can be easily broken down into three categories:

1) Day guests.
2) Evening guests.
3) A standby list in case some people can't make it.

Always stipulate on the invite that you need to know by a certain date if people can't make it so you've got time to fill their space.

Or do what Ryan did and get ruthless! 'There wasn't room to invite everyone during the day so I basically decided that anyone I hadn't met from Fern's family was only invited to the evening do. We didn't have any no-shows on the day but several people I asked to the evening do said they couldn't make it. I do wonder if it's because they weren't invited to the whole day and they had quite a long way to travel. But it's impossible to please everyone. I tended to invite couples during the day and single people in the night-time because they could all come together in a crowd.'

There's always a danger of leaving someone off the guest list, and that danger is elevated when you leave your other half (i.e. Ryan) in charge of it. 'I was definitely nervous Ryan would leave out someone who was key. There was always that risk. Sadly a couple of family members were either forgotten or not invited and it did cause a bit of an argument, which is a real shame. But apart from them everyone I wanted to be there was there so I have to look on the positive side.'

One question that may not be obvious but should be considered when dreaming up your ideal guest list is 'will anyone create a drama or start a fight?' Of course it's not always easy to predict, but if you know someone is likely to get drunk and aggressive or clash with other guests, toughen up and give them a swerve.

Ryan and Fern admit that some of their guests enjoyed the free booze a little too much, which led to some drama. As Ryan says: 'We put on free drinks so one of my friends went a bit mad and smashed a glass on the floor and it hit my best man, Matt. It cut his hand and he had to go to hospital. Then the same mate had a row with the hotel manager and his girlfriend was so horrified she stormed off home. Funnily enough just when it was all happening Fern and I were outside doing an interview and telling the film crew what an amazing day it had been! It wasn't ideal but it gave everyone something to talk about afterwards.'

Please be seated

'If a couple have split up and you've invited both parties it's probably wise to seat them at different tables. And if there is any kind of family feud going on, different ends of the rooms are always preferable.'

Seating plans can be very tricky. Politics can play a part and sometimes you have no choice but to keep certain people apart. If a couple have split up and you've invited both parties it's probably wise to seat them at different tables. And if there is any kind of family feud going on, different ends of the rooms are always preferable.

'The friends side of things was pretty straightforward, but my family are complicated so that made things a bit more difficult,' says Ryan, whose parents split up when he was six. 'My mum and dad were both on the top table, but thankfully they get on well so it was fine. If they hadn't been on the top table I would have had to make a call on whether to sit them together or not and I'm really not sure what I would have decided to do.'

Child's play

'Yes, your guests are hugely important, but at the end of the day they're there to make your day even more special, not stressful!'

Do you want your guests to be able to bring their 'mini-me's' along, or does the thought of them rolling around the dance floor while you're trying to dance to One Direction fill you with horror? There isn't really a right or wrong way to handle this situation. If you decide not to invite children some people may be mildly offended, while others will be thrilled to have a valid excuse to be kid-free.

If you do decide to extend the invitation to children, it's always a good idea to set up a separate area where they can all hang out. Some couples have a kids' table that also includes teens so they keep an eye on the really small ones.

You could also create a play area and hire babysitters so parents can relax and enjoy the day. It doesn't have to cost a fortune. A few games, a TV and some giant cushions work wonders.

If parents want to keep their little ones close it's always a nice idea to provide some colouring-in books (or iPads if money really is no object!) on the tables. Be mindful that if you are inviting youngsters they may need high chairs or booster seats so check in advance that the venue is able to provide them.

Above all, keep in mind that this is your day and it's up to you to decide who you do and don't want to share in your joy. Yes, your guests are hugely important, but at the end of the day they're there to make your day even more special, not stressful!

Highlights from the Show... Seating Plan of Action

Nicole and Sean – Top table-gate

Falling out with your best man can have consequences if you're in sole charge of planning your wedding. When the stresses and strains of sorting the big day comes between groom Sean and his buddy Liam, the communications breakdown leads to a screw-up with the seating plan. The result? No parents on the top table and a bride fit to kill. Despite the oversight, friendship proves as enduring as matrimonial love, and Sean and Liam make up. 'He'll always be my mate,' says the groom, while humbled Liam awards himself just three out of ten for his efforts in supporting the groom.

Adam and Lydia – The tight squeeze

Couples often overlook the fact that the seating at a church ceremony is relatively straightforward. As Adam discovers to his cost, tying the knot in a hotel function room means ensuring enough chairs are in place ahead of the guests. With 100 people filing into a room that normally accommodates 50, he realises what a squeeze it's going to be. 'You lot need to go there,' he says, waving his arms as if directing aircraft on a runway. 'And can we pull the seats forward a bit?' After much last-minute rearranging, everyone has a place and the bride is ready to steal the show.

Nathan & Nicky

Eat, Drink and be Merry

Weddings are all about love, romance, happiness and food, glorious food (oh, and let's not forget the booze)! It's essential to keep your guests well fed and watered during your nuptials, and there are never-ending fabulous catering options.

Nathan and Nicky — The slow burners

'One day I just said to Nicky "come on, let's crack on and get married" in the same way I would say "let's have egg and chips for dinner".'

Nathan and Nicky were 18 and 16 respectively when they met, and Nicky had to wait a whopping ten years for him to pop the question. 'We met in a nightclub and we were dating for quite a while after that,' says Nathan. 'In fact, it was about ten years before I proposed and I did it really lamely. I didn't get down on one knee or anything. One day I just said to Nicky "come on, let's crack on and get married" in the same way I would say "let's have egg and chips for dinner". We'd been together for long enough so it didn't need to be a big gesture. I'm not that soft.'

Policewoman Nicky agrees that it wasn't the most romantic moment of her life. 'The proposal was almost non-existent. He just kind of muttered some words and it was more like a suggestion than a question. He kind of said "do you think we should then?" It wasn't the type of proposal girls dream of. He's not at all romantic. In fact, the show made him look much more romantic than he actually is. I even had to pick my own engagement ring, but that probably was a good thing!'

Nathan, who at the time worked on a farm and was an all-round man's man, was kept in the dark about the possibility of the couple appearing on *Don't Tell The Bride* until after Nicky had sent off the application form. 'I didn't know anything about it until she told me one day that she'd applied. But when we got accepted I thought, "great, I'll have a crack at that". I didn't worry about having to organise anything at all and I actually really enjoyed it. I don't know what the big fuss is about. People take so long to organise a wedding but it was actually quite easy. The only stressful thing was trying to please other people – mainly family – and buying the wedding dress. That was hard because I wanted to get it right and I didn't want to choose something she didn't like. Everything else was water off a duck's back. Basically all you have to do is organise a party, which is easy. I organise things for my job so I found it pretty straightforward.'

Nathan transformed a barn on a farm into a venue fit for a princess for the big day, and Nicky was thrilled with the results. 'It looked lovely and it was actually better than I expected because Nathan never usually pays attention to detail with anything. But he did with the wedding; right down to the "something old, something new, something borrowed, something blue" gift box he left at the wedding dress shop for me. He did really well with the wedding dress too. One of the gowns I'd tried on was a cross between a

'Why not have a chocolate fondue or let people decorate their own cupcakes from a sweet table?'

porn-star dress and one of those knitted loo roll holders your nan has so I was very relieved with his choice. He did really well and it was just the beginning really. Five years on we've got Max, three, and Finny, 18 months, and we're very happy.'

Going the whole hog

The wedding breakfast (so-called because way back in the 18th and 19th centuries couples could only legally get married before midday) is a vital part of the wedding day. Whether you have a sit-down roast dinner or a buffet brimming with sandwiches, you don't want your guests to go hungry. It's always best to have too much rather than too little. Running out of food is a disaster. Having too much isn't.

On the whole, self-catering and buffets will be kinder on the pocket, but keep in mind how much work is involved. It's great if friends and family are willing to help out, but if you're having a large wedding you'll need a lot of them on board to ensure everything is done on time and there's enough of it. A barbecue is always a good option if you're feeling confident about the weather because you can cook on demand.

If you're having your reception in a hotel it's unlikely they'll let you bring in food from outside so make sure you're totally happy with what they can offer. Also check that they can cater for people with allergies/other dietary requirements.

Caterers usually charge per head, which is why it's important to be sure that everyone RSVPs in plenty of time (excuse the pun but you don't want to be forking out for no-shows). Also check whether they do a cheaper kids' menu for the little ones. Talking of allergies, always ask your guests early if they have any special dietary requirements so your caterers have plenty of time to tweak the menu.

If they're having a wedding that starts later on in the day, some couples prefer to serve afternoon tea and then have a buffet in the evening. And you don't have to stick to the standard three course meal if you don't want to. Fish and chips, Indian or Thai menus are good options, and why not have a chocolate fondue or let people decorate their own cupcakes from a sweet table? It's perfect for kids too. Don't forget if you want to save money on dessert you can always serve your wedding cake, which sadly often gets forgotten about.

A traditional day's food and drinking usually looks like this:

- **Welcome drink (with optional canapés)**
- **Three course meal with table wine**
- **Champagne for toasting**
- **Wedding cake**
- **Evening buffet**

Of course you can do as much or as little of this as you want, and if you do decide not to lay on food in the evening it's best to let evening guests know so they can eat before they come. Otherwise you could have some very drunk people on your hands!

Tree-worker Nathan kept things down to earth and simple when it came to his meal. 'There was nothing posh about my dinner. At the time I was working on a farm and the boss gave me a couple of whole pigs to serve. At the start of filming they were running around in a pen and by the end of it they were on our dinner plates. The choice was either a pork dinner, or if you were vegetarian, it was a pork dinner without the pork.'

'The dinner was nice but I wasn't impressed when two pigs' heads were brought out dressed like Nathan and I,' says a horrified Nicky. 'Nathan's pig was wearing a t-shirt and had a chainsaw because of his job, and my pig had a veil on. I'm not sure if Nathan or his boss arranged it but someone obviously thought it would be funny, but it wasn't ideal for the vegetarians. We had a fruit platter and cheese for dessert, and the majority of the wedding cake was made out of cup cakes so people tucked into those too. Weirdly someone stole the top tier of our wedding cake so we didn't get to eat it. I have no idea why but someone clearly liked the look of it.'

Wine not?

'The drunkest person at our wedding was definitely our photographer. He was even too drunk to take any photos so I made him go up in a cherry picker as punishment.'

Booze is a huge part of any wedding, and always has been. Who doesn't want to see their slightly creepy second uncle flailing around a dance floor after too many sherries?

But although you want everyone to have a brilliant time, you don't want people toppling into the cake or starting fights (*see* chapter 10!), so be sure to provide plenty of jugs of water with the meal because that's when people tend to lose track of how much they're drinking.

Some venues will be happy for you to provide your own alcohol, but they often charge a corkage fee so check what that is before you start your online order. Corkage occasionally works out as much as a bottle of wine, so unless you're going all out and serving up top-shelf alcohol it may not be worth it.

Nathan opted for a free bar for his wedding, but unlike some guests, he managed to keep himself in check. 'I laid on £1,000 worth of beer and wine which sounds like a lot but it's amazing how quickly it goes. A lot of people got very drunk, which is standard. Thankfully my hangover wasn't too bad the following day. I've had worse and it was nothing compared to how I felt after the stag do. It was a good thing I wasn't too rough because I had to go back and clean up the barn. I'd also borrowed things like cake stands so I had to take those back to their owners. I wouldn't have been able to do that if I'd been feeling really awful.'

Her manic day meant that Nicky escaped a hangover altogether. 'I didn't have a single drink because I was so busy rushing around. Every time someone gave me a drink I had to go and chat to someone so I kept losing my champagne or wine. The drunkest person at our wedding was definitely our photographer. He was even too drunk to take any photos so I made him go up in a cherry picker as punishment. I told him I wanted photos taken from above and then I left him up there. That taught him a lesson! Aside from him most people were drunk but pretty well behaved and I'm glad we had a free bar because it's a nice thing to do. People already have to pay for their outfit, gift and travel so it's the least you can do. You want everyone to have a good time and not spend a fortune on drinks on top of everything else.'

Local heroes

'People make a big thing of sourcing things locally but why wouldn't you? It's easy and it's cheaper.'

Nathan sourced pretty much everything locally around his native Kidderminster – even the dining tables – and he would recommend that other people to do the same. 'I got as much as I could from local places because it made sense. All the beer was sourced from a local brewery. I went round and did a tour and tried all the drinks and it was absolutely awesome. I went to the local sawmill and cut all of the timber into massive planks and they became our tables. I've still got the head table at home and it's about ten foot long. Five years on I'm still wondering what to do with it! I came across the woman who made our wedding cake when I hired the wedding cars. The guy who worked there said to me "oh, my wife makes wedding cakes" so I got her to do ours. People make a big thing of sourcing things locally but why wouldn't you? It's easy and it's cheaper. The furthest I went was to the next village along from us to buy the wedding dress. I'm sure I saved money by getting things from places nearby.'

Nicky says that her number one piece of advice when it comes to catering – and your day in general – would be to have exactly what you want. 'I would say personalise it to yourself and don't panic about trying to cater to everyone and keep them all happy because you won't be able to do it. It's your day and it's about you, so if you want to serve up mini burgers and chips then you should. The day should be how you want it not how people expect it to be. All the guests said that the minute they walked into our reception they knew it was mine and Nathan's wedding, and it's the little things and those personal touches that make it yours.'

Nathan agrees and also reckons that as long as people get something on their plates and in their glass, they'll be happy. 'To be honest I wouldn't worry too much about the food and drink side of things. Anyone who comes to a wedding doesn't really mind what they get given because it's free. If you're paying for top notch stuff you expect a lot, but you if you're getting it for nothing, you should just enjoy what you get.'

Highlights from the Show... Eat, Drink and be Merry

Rhiana and Rory – The brave face

Hopes run high for Rhiana and her hens when Rory dispatches a minivan to scoop them up. Will it be a night they'll never forget? It certainly will after a two-hour slog, during which the driver requests a whip-round to cover the vehicle hire. Still, Rhiana clings to the belief that her groom will come good, which he does, sort of, when the girls are dropped off outside the couple's favourite eating place: a kebab house where the garlic sauce is a speciality. 'I'm definitely not disappointed,' says Rhiana with a brave little smile. 'I just hope we don't spend the entire evening here.'

Rodney and Paula – Compliments to the cook

Rodney's well aware that his wedding budget might not stretch to cover the day. He needs to do things cheaply without compromising on quality. With little in his pocket but his heart on his sleeve, our groom visits family friend and Caribbean caterer, Beryl, in the hope that he can cut a deal. Not only is Rodney on a shoestring, there's little time left to prepare everything before the wedding. 'You are joking, aren't you?' exclaims Beryl when he sets out his needs. Refusing to take no for an answer, Rodney attempts to close the deal with a simple declaration. 'I love you, Beryl,' he purrs, mentally ticking the food off his to-do list before she draws breath to give in.

Vu and Naomi – The wedding cake cutback

Battling to stay on budget, groom Vu looks to trim the fat from the food bill for his wedding to Naomi. A dream day would be nowhere without a cake, of course, but Vu has a money-saving plan. Together with his mates, he stages a kitchen takeover with a view to creating… wedding cupcakes. '125 grams of everything,' says Vu's mate as they consider the recipe. 'It's easy!' A little while later, looking at the results, the boys' confidence sinks like their creations. 'Six year olds make this with their parents,' the groom reflects bitterly. 'We're three adults and we can't even get it right!'

Colin and Sally – Chocolate for all

A *Willy Wonka*-themed wedding means just one thing – a festival of sweets, and a sea of chocolate. The menu practically writes itself as Colin and co. set to work picking out food with an emphasis on fun. Finally, our groom turns his attention to the main course, otherwise known at this particular big day as 'pudding', while decking out the reception in lollipops, sherbet, toffee and jelly babies, Colin ensures that Sally won't have much trouble in working out what's inspired this special day.

Rosie and Nick – The tasting session

After nearly three weeks assembling his bride's Christmas-themed wedding, Nick and his best man arrive at the wine warehouse. They're tired, stressed and thirsty. Less than perfect conditions, frankly, for some sensible and informed product sampling. 'Would you like to taste some wine today?' asks the assistant, who has to step back in case the duo's heads fall off from such affirmative nodding. Some time later, the boys emerge into the daylight looking worse for wear but with their festive spirits lifted.

Catherine & Richard

Centrepieces: The Good, the Bad and the Ugly

Once upon a time wedding centrepieces were simply an extension of the floral arrangements. But nowadays it's not unusual to see balloons, love hearts or even fish bowls sitting proudly in the middle of a table. As for favours? Old-school sugared almonds are still the top choice for traditionalists but nowadays literally anything, from candles to cupcakes, goes.

Richard and Catherine — An early toast

'We got hot dogs for the walk back to our hotel and sat on a bench in the middle of the street to finish them off. The next thing I knew Richard was down on one knee.'

Richard and Catherine met when they were both 18 and studying at Derby University. They'd only been at uni for a matter of days before fate – and a breakfast faux pas – brought them together. As Richard explains: 'I lived above Catherine in halls and one morning she was making breakfast and she burnt her toast. The fire alarm went off and the entire building was evacuated with most people, including me, still wearing their pyjamas. Everyone had terrible hangovers so they weren't terribly happy with her.'

'We spoke briefly that day and I thought he was cute,' Catherine admits. 'He used to come down to my floor and play video games with one of his mates, so I'd make excuses to go and hang out with them. One night we ended up getting together and we dated for the whole of uni. After we both graduated, Richard moved back to London and I went back to Glasgow and we started having a long-distance relationship, which involved a lot of trips on National Express and the Megabus. Eventually we realised that 500 miles was a bit too far to keep things going so Richard moved to Glasgow.

'I kept saying, "I could do a much better job of organising a wedding", so Catherine challenged me to apply as a joke and I took her up on it.'

When he got offered a job in Leamington Spa we relocated to there, and we now live in Coventry.'

The couple were together for three and a half years before they got engaged. And, although Catherine didn't think twice about saying yes when Richard popped the all-important question, she wasn't overly enamoured with how he did it. 'The way Richard proposed wasn't romantic at all,' she laughs. 'We were on holiday in Barcelona, so it starts off well, but then it goes downhill. We watched Arsenal play and then went to an arcade to play some games. We got hot dogs for the walk back to our hotel and sat on a bench in the middle of the street to finish them off. The next thing I knew Richard was down on one knee. When I look back at the night all I think is "Arsenal, air hockey and hot dogs". But to be fair to him he had picked a lovely ring and it fitted perfectly. I don't know why he chose to do it at that moment and in that place. He says it was a mixture of alcohol and nerves.'

Purple peril

It was while they were watching a couple called Paula and Rodney get married on the first series of *Don't Tell The Bride* that they got the idea to apply for the show themselves. 'Rodney was talking about putting up a marquee in the car park of a pub and I was taking the mickey out of him,' explains Richard. 'I kept saying, "I could do a much better job of organising a wedding", so Catherine challenged me to apply as a joke and I took her up on it. We didn't think we had a chance of being chosen for the programme and it was only when we were about to go on camera for the first time that the reality of it what we were about to do kicked in.'

Richard, who is general manager of a hospital, enlisted the help of his best man, Phil, and his brother, Matthew, to keep things on track. 'They were good moral support and they made it enjoyable because they had a sense of humour about

everything. I spent the entire three weeks leading up to the wedding getting up at 8am and going to bed at 3am. In the end I got the venue, Wroxhall Abbey in Warwickshire, due to a cancellation and it was such a relief. There were a few tricky moments here and there but I really didn't find it that stressful really. I had a lot of fun.'

Richard, whose dad is from Guyana, arranged to have a Scottish-Caribbean theme to celebrate his and Catherine's cultures. But while he managed to stay relatively calm, there were some stressful moments for learning-mentor Catherine – especially when she clapped eyes on the invites. 'I'm usually in charge of organising things, so it was terrifying letting Richard have all the control for once. There were times when I nearly caved in, especially when the wedding invitation arrived. It was covered in purple polka dots and had a garish tartan ribbon tied around it, which I hated. It didn't bode well. I'm not a fan of purple anyway and at that moment everything became very real and the panic set in. Thankfully it wasn't a reflection on the rest of the wedding. Richard chose a gorgeous dress for me. I was worried he was going to pick something really flouncy but thankfully he didn't. Although it was a bit more blingy than I would have chosen it was also very simple and I cried when I first saw it. I wasn't quite as keen on the bridesmaids' dresses – which were purple – but they did grow on me.'

'After the meal we were all called out to the terrace and Richard was standing there in a Hawaiian shirt playing along with a steel band... Some of our guests started limbo dancing, and when it got really dark we released sky lanterns which looked beautiful.'

The couple married on a May bank holiday in 2009, and Catherine couldn't believe Richard managed to secure the incredible venue at such short notice. 'The place was amazing. When I arrived there was a piper playing and it was so beautiful. I was so pleased to see Richard. I gave him a massive hug when I got to the end of the aisle. After the meal we were all called out to the terrace and Richard was standing there in a Hawaiian shirt playing along with a steel band. He had been taking secret lessons in the run-up to the wedding. Some of our guests started limbo dancing, and when it got really dark we released sky lanterns which looked beautiful. I am so appreciative of all the hard work he put in. It was incredible.'

Centre of attention

Centrepieces can be the perfect way to express your personality, and because they're such an integral part of the table plan you want them to wow. Helium balloons with long ribbon strings are a great option because they won't hamper anyone's view, while glass bowls filled with fairy lights give everything a magical glow.

'We ended up with our centrepieces by sheer coincidence,' says Richard. 'My best man, my brother and I originally went to Hobbycraft and chose really thin, tall vases and some very tall purple flowers to go in them. I was standing in the

queue to pay when I looked and suddenly thought "they look terrible". I also realised that they were so big people wouldn't have been able to see each other across the table. My best man and I later spotted some mirrored cubes in a florist. They were using them as decoration, but I really liked them so I asked if we could buy a load and they became our centrepieces.'

Catherine, who is head of year at a school in Birmingham, is incredibly pleased Richard changed his mind about his first choice. 'Tall vases with tall flowers – what was he thinking? I'm so relieved he didn't have those. I loved the mirrored cubes though. We've still got some of them at home and they're very handy. We've got one in the kitchen that has our dishwasher tablets in it. I was really impressed with the centrepieces overall. Richard put thistles in amongst the flowers to reflect my Scottish roots so they felt really personal.'

Do me a favour

It's long been tradition for guests to receive a small gift as a thank you for sharing in a bride and groom's joy. These are usually left on the tables so guests receive them as they sit down to enjoy the wedding breakfast.

The most popular wedding favour is sugared almonds. The custom is thought to have originated way back in the 13th century, when five almonds were given to each person to represent fertility, longevity, wealth, health and happiness.

Fast-forward to the modern day and favours have grown in popularity and come in all shapes and sizes. There's something to suit everyone's taste, from the handmade to the decadent.

'Mid-budget ideas include scented soaps, bath bombs, USB sticks with a selection of wedding photos, CDs of music from the day, chocolates, fridge magnets and printed marshmallows.'

Mid-budget ideas include scented soaps, bath bombs, USB sticks with a selection of wedding photos, CDs of music from the day, chocolates, fridge magnets and printed marshmallows. Miniature bottles of alcohol are always very welcome, and it's a nice idea to choose something that guests can slip into their after-dinner coffee.

If money really is no object, you could gift silver picture frames with a wedding photo inside, candles with personalised labels, or whisky and wine glasses with inscriptions on.

If you want to save some pennies, you could make your own fairy cakes or sweets, and buy everyone a £1 scratchcard each.

If you want to give back, you could make a donation to a charity of your choice on behalf of your guests, or look online for charities that will make up wedding favours for you for a fee.

Much like he did with his centrepieces, Richard came up with the idea for his favours by mistake. 'I didn't want to go with the usual sugared almonds because, even though I'm probably one of the only people who eats them at a wedding, I know not everyone is keen. One day I ended up in an old sweet shop with some friends buying a load of pick and mix, and inspiration hit, so I bought a load of little love heart sweets and put them in pouches. They didn't cost a lot and I was really pleased with how they looked. I love going to weddings where things aren't as you'd expect. Some friends of ours hired an ice-cream van and the favour was a ticket, which you could take outside and exchange for anything you wanted. Another mate of ours had an Alice in Wonderland theme. Her centrepieces were teapots and her favours were glass "drink me" bottles with shots inside them.'

While she doesn't dislike them, Catherine was glad Richard decided to give sugared almonds a swerve. 'I'm very pleased he decided against them. I was a flower girl for my auntie 25 years ago and she had them then, so they're definitely quite old fashioned now. They do look pretty and they're nice if you're having a very traditional day but I do think it's good to do something different. My sister had tablet at her wedding – which is a bit like fudge and very Scottish – and people loved it. Some friends of ours made their own cake pops as favours and they were brilliant. Our daughter was too young to eat hers so Richard swiped hers too. My mum and my stepdad John made sweets for the girls and provided miniature bottles of whisky for the men, which looked really cute. It's so nice when people make the effort to do something unusual.'

Bonny babies

'Just think: if I hadn't been so rubbish in the kitchen back then none of this may have happened!'

Richard and Catherine are now nicely settled with their four-year-old daughter, Alyssa, and their new arrival, Theo. The couple still laugh about how they got together. 'It's crazy to think all of this came about because I burnt a piece of toast!' says Catherine. 'Just think: if I hadn't been so rubbish in the kitchen back then none of this may have happened!'

Highlights from the Show... Centrepieces: The Good, the Bad and the Ugly

Ian and Hayley – Fishy business

Hardworking Hayley is plunged out of her depth when she hands over control of her big day to a man with a crazy underwater plan. After a sub-aqua ceremony in the swimming pool, and back on dry land, our groom plans to keep the theme from sinking when the guests take their seats for the reception. 'You've got fish on the tables!' declares Hayley, admiring the exotic cylindrical tanks that Ian has arranged as centrepieces. 'I love it. That's absolutely brilliant!'

Matt and Rian – The cut-price centrepieces

With a budget to make wedding dreams come true, Matt only goes and blows a whacking big chunk of it on a stag night in Vegas. With the outgoings mounting, and his heart set on revolving the day around a nostalgic theme, he aims to make cutbacks without compromising on quality. As a result, Matt takes his search for table centrepieces to a car boot sale, and walks away with a bunch of Belgian beer jugs for just £2. Lovely jubbly, and a clear example of what not to tell the bride. Ever.

Lauren and Charles – Out of this world (part 1)

The pressure is on for sci-fi fanatic Charles as he tries to impress his classy bride-to-be. While Lauren holds out hope for a tasteful and traditional wedding, Charles sets his sights on going where no groom has gone before. With a futuristic reception populated by robot waiters, he decides that flowers have no place as centrepieces on the top tables. Why go floral when glowing electrostatic orbs will spark the atmosphere he's been seeking? 'I'm quite happy with these,' says Charles, on first playing with his balls, but will they light up Lauren's day in quite the same way?

Lauren and Charles – Out of this world (part 2)

Charles might've sorted the centrepieces, but staging a convincing sci-fi themed wedding is still set to cost him the earth. When the bride finally lays eyes on a reception that could double as a space canteen, she's overwhelmed – in a good way – and recognises just how much blood, sweat and most of the budget has gone into making this day feel out of this world. Having got away with showing Lauren his space-age cake, Charles reaches the favours. It may have cost nothing to pen an individual message for each guest, but every word comes from the bottom of his heart. And if that's not enough, he's given every one of them a cardboard mask. Just what every wedding guest expects.

Ian & Hayley
Flower Power

From bouquets to buttonholes, floral displays are a huge part of any celebration and help to make the day bright and beautiful. Beads, buttons and feathers can all be included to give things a more contemporary feel, and there are plenty of ways to keep things cheap but very cheerful!

Ian and Hayley — Wat-er couple

'I went for a swim and when I got out of the sea I pulled the ring out of my pocket and popped the question.'

Ian may have used a very cheesy chat-up line to try and woo Hayley, but it clearly did the trick because seven years on they're happier than ever. 'I was training at my local leisure centre and at the time Hayley was working there as a personal trainer. I used the ultimate chat up line "can you stretch my hamstrings please?" and amazingly it worked. We were both 23 and we went out for a date on Hayley's birthday, and that was it. We were together for three years before I proposed. We went on holiday to Turkey and I'd already asked her parents' permission beforehand. We went down to the beach on the first day just as the sun was setting. I went for a swim and when I got out of the sea I pulled the ring out of my pocket and popped the question.'

'It was all very lovely and romantic but I was horrified when I found out he'd been swimming with the ring in his pocket. Imagine if he'd lost it!' says a still concerned Hayley. 'He'd bought a couple of mini bottles of champagne so he was clearly very confident that I was going to say yes – which of course I did! We both sat and watched the sun go down, and then we went to our favourite restaurant for a nice meal. It was so lovely.'

'I was shocked, pleased and a little bit scared when we found out we'd been accepted. Mainly scared because I was about to hand over all of the wedding power to Ian and I had no idea what he would have in mind.'

H2-NO

It was her mum who encouraged primary school teacher Hayley to apply for *Don't Tell The Bride*. Ian was on a late shift at work when Hayley filled out the application form so he was bombarded with a series of random questions via text and was left feeling very confused. 'I sent the form off but really didn't expect to hear anything back,' admits Hayley. 'I was shocked, pleased and a little bit scared when we found out we'd been accepted. Mainly scared because I was about to hand over all of the wedding power to Ian and I had no idea what he would have in mind.'

Some might say she had every reason to be scared. Considering Hayley is usually the main organiser in the relationship she was taking some risk. Ian knew immediately that he wanted to do away with convention and plan a wedding unlike any other, one that involved water. A lot of water. 'We got married in a swimming pool at Pelthorne Leisure Centre in Staines. It was completely crazy,' says Hayley shaking her head at the memory. 'I didn't know what to think when I realised what was happening and my initial thought was "what about my hair and make-up? They've taken forever to do!" But actually the whole day ran so smoothly. I should have trusted him really. I'm usually the one who keeps everything in check. If Ian cleans the house I'll go round cleaning up after him because he's a bit rubbish, but he'd thought of everything.'

Thankfully that included a grooming squad. 'He had a hair and make-up artists on standby to make sure I looked presentable for the reception, which was a big relief,' says Hayley. 'I had visions of myself looking like a drowned rat during our first dance but he had another dress ready for me to put on. That day taught me that there's more than one way to make things work. It's not something I would ever have imagined doing but it was so brilliant. I know some people may think it's very weird to get married in a swimming pool but I honestly felt like any other bride would. I was crying as I was swimming down the aisle and I had to clear my goggles so I could see where I was going. I also lost a flipper halfway through the vows so I felt like a Cinderella bride. I've always thought I was a mermaid in a former life and I felt so special that day. It may not be for everyone and I'm sure some people think it's a totally crazy thing to do but when I look back on it I wouldn't have had it any other way.'

The pool itself already held special memories for the couple because it was where Hayley taught Ian to swim. 'Hayley always says she is more comfortable in the water so it was the sentimental side of being in the water I wanted to do,' Ian explains.

Coming up roses

Flowers can make or break the look of a wedding, and it's one of the things couples take the most time over. They can either set the colour scheme or fit in with it. Either way, much like a contestant on *The X Factor*, you want your blooms to 'smash it'.

The main floral arrangements you have to think about are:

- **Bride's bouquet**
- **Bridesmaids' bouquets**
- **Gents' buttonholes**
- **Flower girls' baskets**
- **Church flowers**
- **Reception flowers**
- **Centrepieces**

Bouquets provide a great opportunity to be creative, and they don't have to be all about the flowers. If you want something a bit different why not try:

- **Fairy lights to give a gorgeous glow.**
- **Shells, which are especially pertinent if you're tying the knot by the sea.**
- **Pom-poms, which look cute and cool.**
- **Dried flowers, which have a huge sense of romance about them.**
- **Spray-painting your bouquet silver or gold – just because!**
- **Feathers, for a fun, flirty look.**
- **A bouquet of lollipops (these will also come in handy for the kids at the reception).**
- **Fir cones. Lovely if you're having a winter wedding, and even better when spray-painted (see above!).**
- **Fabric flowers. A huge benefit is that they'll last forever.**
- **Buttons and beads. You can guarantee you'll have a posy like no other.**

Choosing the right flowers can be complex, but it was even more of a challenge for Ian because he had to source ones that would work in water as well as out of it. 'I'm not a big fan of flowers really and I did pretty well considering it was the first bunch of flowers I'd ever bought for Hayley,' Ian confesses. 'I had a lot of help from the lovely lady in the florist and I was really pleased with my choices. Of course, for the bouquet Hayley had in the pool I had to find something that would survive being plunged into water. My best men and I went to pretty much every flower shop in the Surrey area and eventually we found a lovely plastic arrangement. I also added in what I can only describe as some rainbow-coloured bits of tinsel to make them look more glamorous. It may not sound that pretty but it worked really well. We also went to a garden centre and bought a plain rose arch and attached fake flowers and organza to it so we could have that in the water too.'

Ian wanted the arrangements for the reception, which was held at Lythe Hill Hotel in Haslemere, to match in with the underwater theme, so he gave the foliage a marine feel. 'Hayley's favourite colour is pink, so all of the flowers were pink but the foliage was green and I tried to get things that looked like underwater plants. I also added in some fairy lights for extra glamour because I knew Hayley would love that. Each of the bridesmaids had a single rose attached to a light up star-shaped wand to emulate starfish.'

Blooming expensive

It seems when it comes to wedding flowers you can put on a price on beauty and it's sensible to set aside a fair whack to splash on your sprays. If you're keen to keep costs down, some savvy money-saving tips include:

- Opt for single stems. Simple, effective and very reasonable.
- Use wild flowers. Be sure to check beforehand where you can and can't pick them as you could be prosecuted. For instance, flowers that grow in council parks, community gardens, verges, nature reserves and roundabouts are legally protected (the roundabout option sounds quite perilous, to be fair). Also always check what you're picking because some botanicals can be poisonous, while specific plants and flowers, such as lady's slipper orchid and sandwort, are also off limits as they're protected under the 1981 Wildlife and Countryside Act. You can find a comprehensive list of what you are and aren't allowed to pick online. In an ideal world you'd grow your own flowers in your own back garden, then as long as you give yourself permission to pilfer them you'll be totally fine.
- Use extra greenery. It's generally much cheaper than the flowers themselves.
- Choose cheaper flowers. It may be obvious, but having daffodils instead of roses really can save you a small fortune.
- Haggle. There are loads of florists out there who would love your business so look around for the best deal, or negotiate one.
- Buy flowers that are in season as they're always more reasonable.
- Be flexible about what you want. Florists may be able to source something similar to your dream flower at a fraction of the price.
- Use fake flowers. These often work out much cheaper and last a lot longer!

When it came to his flower costings, Ian felt rather, ahem, out of his depth. 'I was shocked by how much the flowers were. I budgeted about £70 in total which looking back is absolutely ridiculous. I had managed the budget really well with everything else so thankfully I had a bit of money left over, most of which went on the floral arrangements. I can't remember the exact figure but when you add it all up it came to a lot. I estimated most other things really well but that was where I came unstuck.'

'All the things Ian did worked because the flowers were beautiful. Even the plastic ones!' laughs Hayley. 'I'm glad he spent more on them because it was well worth it.'

Floral wisdom

Having learned a lot from his first flower-buying experience, Nathan has some good recommendations for fellow wedding planners. 'If I had to give everyone advice about flowers it would be to shop around and try and get a good deal if you're going to bulk-buy. But don't underestimate the cost, because however much you think it will be, you can guarantee it will be

'Don't be worried about walking out of a shop because you don't feel like they're going to do what you want them to.'

more. Another thing I would say is stick to your guns. I went to a couple of florists who wanted to stick to a certain formula. They clearly thought 'oh, it's a wedding, we'll do what we do for every other one'. I had to really stand my ground and tell them exactly what I wanted. Don't be worried about walking out of a shop because you don't feel like they're going to do what you want them to. There will always be other shops and someone somewhere who is willing to help you. The florist needs to be able to buy into what you're doing. The ones who helped me out the most and supported me were the people who were most open-minded. And at the end of the day they were the ones who got my money! Finally, get creative. I added in things like the tinsel to Hayley's bouquet and I made the arch myself, and those things would have cost a lot more if I'd paid someone to do it.'

Making a splash

'Everything came together brilliantly,' reflects recruitment manager Ian. 'Looking back at our wedding day I still can't believe I pulled it off. From splashing around in the sea just before I proposed to getting married underwater, our marriage has had a very watery theme.'

Highlights from the Show... Flower Power

Liam and Lynn – What in the world?

'Oh, my God! What's he doing?' A delivery of flowers on her wedding day is enough to put Lynn and her bridesmaids on high alert. Instead of your standard carnations and roses, Liam has opted for the kind of weird and wonderful flora you might find on some faraway planet investigated by Captain James T Kirk and crew. Grasping a posy comprising of weird yellow orbs and flowers with what look like pink tendrils unfolding from them, the bride is left in no doubt of the kind of wedding theme Liam has in mind. 'Aliens,' she says, and takes a fortifying swig of champagne.

Cameron and Sarah – Floral warning

Planning a dream day for your bride is tough enough, but what if her sister has already bagged all the best bits for her own forthcoming wedding? Like a hawk with a headache, Sarah's sister, Katie, is watching every move that Cameron makes. 'It does panic me a bit that he's going to pick up on the things that I want,' she says casually, though it's one of Sarah's bridesmaids who spells out Katie's central concern. 'She's obsessed with her flowers. If it were the same flowers, I think she'd go mental.' Wisely, Cameron makes his floral selection from the opposite end of the colour spectrum. The result? A happy day for one and all, including sister, Katie, who recognises that love, fun, family and friends is what makes the perfect wedding.

Josh and Stacie – Say it with flowers

Josh decides to dispatch his brother to present Stacie with a floral invitation to their Jamaican/Irish wedding. The young man is keen to do the job, but lacks a deep briefing in exactly what he's presenting. 'This is the bird of paradise representing you,' he begins, gesturing at one of the two flowers as he focuses hard on remembering his lines. 'And the shamrock, representing Josh.' Stacie looks stunned. 'Is this the colours?' she asks, which prompts Josh's brother to retreat by several paces. 'I'm saying nothing,' he says, before making a hasty exit. Still, Stacie is keen to seek some meaning from the flowers in her hand. 'Is a bird of paradise a hint?' she asks excitedly. 'Are we getting married abroad?' Erm, no.

Dan and Mark – Button it

The big day dawns and the pressure is starting to mount. Dan has run himself ragged in making sure everything is in place. Meanwhile, Mark has found it tough to release control and let his partner do all the planning. In a short while, he'll discover that Dan has made his dreams come true. Until then, he takes one look at the very big flower intended as a buttonhole and instructs his bridesmaid to get on the phone to Dan's best man – stressed out Steve. 'That's the flower Mark's meant to be wearing,' Steve confirms, in no mood for any last-minute change of plan. 'If he doesn't wear it, that's his choice, but he won't be matching Dan.' That told them.

Hywel & Beca

Get Me to the Church on Time

The church is booked, the dress is bought and the vows have been rehearsed. Now all your need to do is make sure you make it to the church in style and on time. From a Harley to horseback, there are numerous ways you can travel in style.

Hywel and Beca — The Boozy Besties

'We got together, started living together, got engaged and got married within the space of two years. And we're still going strong.'

Civil servants Hywel and Beca first met when they were at secondary school. Although they were aware of each other, they hung around in different social groups, so it took them another ten years to actually get together. As Hywel says, 'I always knew who Beca was because she's a very attractive lady. We didn't move in the same circles when we were younger, and then when we got to our late teens Beca left to join the RAF and I went to university in Cardiff so we didn't see each other for years. We both moved back to South Wales in our mid-twenties and that's when our paths crossed again.'

'We bumped into each other in a pub and we had a couple of drunken encounters,' laughs Beca. 'The timing never seemed right for us to properly get together, but then one day something clicked and we started officially seeing each other. We were together for about a year before he proposed. We were both very drunk at a Blur gig in Hyde Park so I didn't take him seriously at first. Then a few days later he broached the subject again and I thought "okay then, it will be fun if we stay together forever".'

Hywel admits that his initial proposal was largely beer-fuelled, but it spurred him on to do things formally. 'The gig proposal was kind of unofficial. I got a bit carried away and seized the moment and got down on one knee. Beca kind of laughed it off, but I knew I really wanted her to be my wife so when we got back to South Wales I spoke to her son Alex about it and also got permission from her father. Thankfully she said yes when I asked again.'

Hywel already had his eye on an engagement ring. But he made the sensible decision of letting Beca cast her eyes over it before he handed over his cold, hard cash. 'It's made of Welsh gold and it has "cariad" inscribed inside, which means "love" in Welsh. We've also got matching wedding bands that have the same inscription. Beca had been married before and I'd been in long-term relationships so I think we were both at that age where we knew what we wanted and the type of person we wanted to be with so everything happened really quickly. We got together, started living together, got engaged and got married within the space of two years. And we're still going strong.'

Glasto glamour

'At first I was like "are you serious? You're going to organise my wedding?"'

Hywel was the one who applied for *Don't Tell The Bride* after catching glimpses of the show when Beca was watching it. 'One day I asked her how the show worked. When she explained, I joked that I'd love it do it so Beca challenged me to put my money where my mouth is. Once we got accepted I started thinking about what I could do to make it really special. I knew I wanted it to be music-related so that gave me loads of options.'

Although Beca was initially concerned about how her big day would pan out, she had every faith Hywel would make it amazing. 'At first I was like "are you serious? You're going to organise my wedding?" But Hywel is a good laugh and he always comes up smelling of roses whatever he does. I knew it would be good fun and that he wouldn't do anything really stupid. All I hoped was that it would be a classy affair and maybe incorporate something a bit vintagey. I had this vision of us having a lovely cocktail party-themed wedding.'

Hywel, however, had other ideas. In keeping with his music theme, he mulled over the possibility of the couple trying the knot in a concert venue before deciding on a festival feel. 'I wanted to do something outdoors and the plan was to bring a bit of Glastonbury to South Wales. It tied in well with our relationship because Beca and I have been to Glastonbury together a few times and had some really good times there. Also, I first proposed at a gig so it was very poignant.'

Camping it up

'Campervans are always popular at festivals so I decided to hire one of those and it worked really well...'

The wedding, held at Dyffryn Springs in Cardiff, boasted a giant marquee, live bands and tables named after groups. Even the caterers were called Strawberry Field. And when it came to the transport, Hywel made sure it was in keeping with the rest of the day. 'I wanted a cool, different way to get Beca to the venue. Campervans are always popular at festivals so I decided to hire one of those and it worked really well. I really liked the fact that so many people could travel in it with her so she was surrounded by people who meant to a lot to her.'

'I had to smile when it pulled up,' Beca grins. 'Hywel hired the campervan from a guy who lives near us and he also hires out Volkswagen Beetles that have different names, including one called Elvis. He says that quite often the bride and her dad will travel in a Beetle and the rest of the wedding party will go in the campervan, which is really funky. I wasn't expecting a stretch limo because I knew it would be too traditional for Hywel, but I was half thinking he may choose a classic car like a Bentley or a Rolls Royce. I actually really liked the campervan because it was cool, and

because it was so big it meant that there was plenty of room for my dad, all my bridesmaids and my son, Alex. That made it really special. The only problem was it was very, very slow. It didn't go over 30 miles an hour so it took forever to get to the venue!'

Hywel's only regret is that he didn't hire a VW for himself. 'I stayed in a B&B around the corner from the venue so my best friend's girlfriend gave me a lift in her Land Rover on the morning of the wedding. If the budget had stretched to it I would definitely have got a second campervan for me though. I was lucky enough to go for a little jaunt in Beca's in between the ceremony and the reception, and it was good fun to have a drive around the lanes. It was also great driving it into the reception with Beca at my side. That was a great moment.'

Keep on truckin'

'Personally I would just advise people to ensure as many guests as possible see it so they get their money's worth!'

There are no limits when it comes to selecting your own mode of transport for your special day. But, like a good boy scout, make sure you're prepared.

It's always an idea to factor transport into your budget early on because it can end up being very pricey.

If you have your heart set on a classic car – popular models include Bentley, Aston Martin, Porsche, Mercedes, Limousine, Jaguar and Rolls Royce – book early to avoid disappointment, as they're the first vehicles to get snapped up during crazy wedding season. Ideally they should be secured with a deposit around six months before the big day.

If you want to take a leaf out of Hywell's book and roll up in something a bit more unconventional you could always follow in Jackie's terrifying footsteps and skydive into your ceremony, or how about hiring a helicopter, motorbike, boat (this only really works if you're near water!), horse and carriage, bicycles, monster truck or a tractor? And how about laying on a classic red bus to ferry your guests around? Not only will they get a chance to get to know each other, but you could even leave mini bottles of wine on each seat so they can get the party started early.

'I was a bridesmaid at my best friend's wedding and she had a '69 Dodge Charger, which is the same car they have in *The Dukes of Hazzard*,' says Beca. 'She saw someone driving around in it one day so she followed them and flashed her lights to get them to stop. Eventually they did and she asked the owner if he'd drive her to her wedding. He wasn't a proper chauffeur or anything but amazingly he agreed. There are so many options when it comes to transport but you have to go for what you want and not worry about what anyone else thinks. If you want something that's a bit out there go for it. It's your day and the quirkier it is the more it will get talked about afterwards.'

Hywel reckons you don't have to spend a fortune on travelling from A to B – especially when sometimes your guests don't even get to appreciate it.

'I've been to a lot of weddings where you don't even get to see the transport so it's crazy that people spend so much money on it. But I guess it's more about the bride and her wedding party than the guests, so they have to do whatever makes them happy. Personally I would just advise people to ensure as many guests as possible see it so they get their money's worth! The campervan was actually really reasonable to hire, and everyone really liked it so it shows you don't have to spend a fortune.'

Something else to consider transport-wise is parking. Make sure there is ample room for guests to leave their cars at both the ceremony and reception or advise about local car parks. If your wedding is in a small village or a built-up area it's always nice to alert local residents that there may be more traffic and noise than usual. You could even look into hiring out people's driveways/farmer's fields as an overspill car park.

Rock on

As a little-known pop combo called The Beatles once sang, 'All You Need is Love', and now they've Come Together (sorry), Hywel and Beca are happier than ever. As well as Alex, who is now 12, but the couple have a baby girl called Isla, and from what Beca says it sounds like their music-filled day has had quite an effect on their son. 'Isla is amazing and Alex is a really cool dude. He's in a band now and he plays the guitar and drums, and he does gigs and all sorts. He's such a big music fan.'

It may have been several years ago now, but the couple still get recognised off the back of their memorable TV appearance. 'Because we come from a small town it was big news. I didn't realise how many people watch the programme but we got recognised constantly and we still do now,' Beca laughs. 'People are always so lovely. I know I'm not a big celebrity like Kate Moss but some of the things that have happened are so funny. We even had a checkout opened up especially for us in Tesco, and when we go on holiday or to Glastonbury people came up to talk to us about the show all the time.'

'Our wedding was just incredible. The sun was shining and all of our friends and family were there with us, and we've been on top of the world ever since,' says a very happy Hywel. 'We already had a very happy family and when Isla came along she bought even more joy to us. Alex is a brilliant big brother and it's amazing to have a son and a daughter. We're about to buy our first house together and it's happy days all round.'

Liam & Lynn

The Night(mare) Before

A wedding might appear to be nothing more than a public declaration of love and commitment to one another. In reality, it can often require a strategic master plan that would outwit a military general. From the moment you set the date, a countdown begins and there's no going back. So, how do you cope when doubts creep in about your vision for the big day? It's only natural that you might reflect on the wisdom of your decisions when faced with compromises and setbacks that occur in the run-up. With so much pressure on your shoulders, what can you do to stop yourself from hauling the duvet over your head and refusing to get out of bed?

In many ways, the preparation stages are a strong test of character. It demands nerves of steel as much as focus, creativity and drive. Some people thrive on the challenge. Others can feel out of their comfort zone at times. Then there are those who find themselves questioning if they're doing the right thing at all. If you're planning something ambitious, or even just plain weird, then a moment is bound to come when you ask yourself if you're out of your mind. Without doubt, it's a stressful time, and managing any wobbles that arise is all part of the process.

The good news is that you're not the first couple to plan a wedding. Millions of people have gone through it, faced moments of uncertainty and even crisis, but come out smiling on the other side.

Liam and Lynn — Abducted by aliens

'Just for one day,' declares Liam, reflecting on the concept behind his wedding, 'I wanted Lynn to be a part of my mind.' This might sound like a sweet and heartfelt gesture from a groom to his bride, and indeed it is. What sets it apart is the fact that this livewire electrician from Surrey is obsessed with UFO's and the conspiracy theories surrounding the subject. 'Anything out of the ordinary appeals to me,' he says. 'People say that makes me strange, and maybe it's true. I just hoped my plans would give a true picture of what I'm really like.'

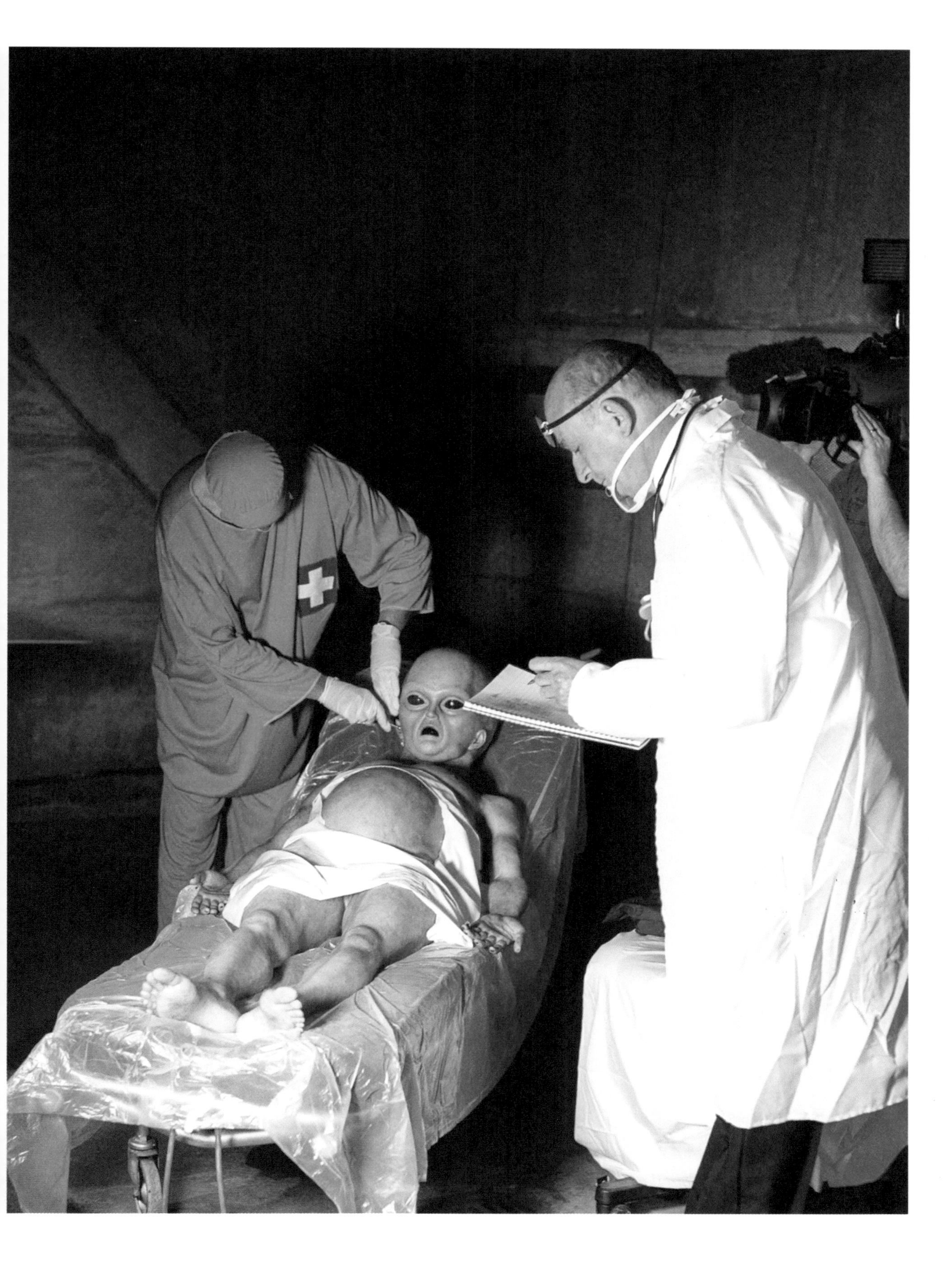

In many ways, however, level-headed legal secretary Lynn already had a pretty good idea. 'He's a weirdo,' she smiles. 'Everyone says that about Liam. But at the same time he's also the life and soul of any party. You never get bored talking to him. Nor can you predict what he'll do next, especially not at a wedding!'

The couple met at a music festival in 2009. Now, they're rocking a happy family unit with a young daughter and Lynn's son from a previous relationship. Determined to seal the deal, and with his proposal accepted, Liam had every intention of giving his bride a day she'd never forget. That Lynn knew her fiancé so well meant she had some concerns about what he might have in store. 'In my mind, I knew that he'd plan something unusual,' she says, 'but I didn't think he'd take things too far. For my benefit, I thought he might keep things traditional. At the very least, I hoped my dress would be nice…'

Lynn also admits she had a second worry about his ability to pull off the perfect wedding. 'Liam is really unorganised,' she says. 'In a way there's never been a need for him to get it together because I do all the organising for him.' It's an observation that Liam doesn't dispute. 'Lynn is a human list,' he adds, 'but I was determined not to let her down.'

> **'Unaware of her fiancé's plan to host a ceremony and reception that resembled a large-scale UFO cover-up, complete with men in black, alien autopsies, strange flashing lights and smoke machines…'**

Under pressure

All weddings come with sky-high expectation. It's often called 'the perfect day' or 'the dream day' for good reason. Everyone from the bride down wants to feel sure that they'll look back on the event with nothing but happy memories. As a result, it's easy to commit one hundred percent to the planning and yet still feel as if you're falling short. 'As things took shape in my head I kept asking myself, "is Lynn going to be OK with this?"' says Liam. 'I knew she wanted a fairy tale wedding, but that's just not me. At the same time, even if I had gone down the traditional route, there's just so much work to do in setting everything up that I'd still have questioned whether it would work out alright. With so much weight on your shoulders to get things right, it's just a natural reaction.'

Unaware of her fiancé's plan to host a ceremony and reception that resembled a large-scale UFO cover-up, complete with men in black, alien autopsies, strange flashing lights and smoke machines, Lynn could only hope that Liam wouldn't crack under the strain. 'It's a big day and I didn't want him to ruin it,' she says. Knowing full well that his extra-terrestrial concept might not have been top of Lynn's wish list, Liam admits to being scared of how she might react. 'She can be quite fiery, and the last thing I wanted to do was upset her,' he says. 'The same went for the guests. With my plan for us to marry in front of an alien minister, I even worried whether some people might find it distasteful!'

Taking the strain

'I was with my brother and best mate, and we were looking around an underground bunker in the woods. It was dark, mouldy, claustrophobic and smelly...'

Doubts can seep into all aspects of the planning process. Whether you've been forced to make changes to stay on-budget, or you're simply fretting that you might have bitten off more than you can chew, it's very easy to sense your confidence and enthusiasm start to fade. Even if you're committed to the whole prospect of getting married, how can you cope when the going gets tough? What strategies can you call upon to see you through those moments, and stay true to your ultimate aim: a wedding day like no other?

As many couples who have been through the process will say, it's a time when you often need to turn to friends and family for support. 'I started feeling the strain when we checked out the first location,' says Liam. 'I was with my brother and best mate, and we were looking around an underground bunker in the woods. It was dark, mouldy, claustrophobic and smelly. In my mind, I was struggling to transform it in into this amazing venue. It was beginning to leave me feeling desperate, because basically the place was a dump, and that's when I needed those guys. They might've spent most of their time laughing, but it helped me see the light as we left and focussed on finding something more practical.' Meanwhile, together with her friends and

family, Liam's bride had been spending her time touring her ideal kind of venues. 'We went to see all these lovely places, but I just knew that I wouldn't be getting anything like that,' she says. 'Weirdly, I didn't mind too much, and everyone with me could see that for themselves. At the end of the day, I really loved Liam and just wanted to get married. The rest was up to him.'

Believe in yourself

In the build-up to a wedding, it can be comforting to surround yourself with people you trust. With the right support network, you know that you can turn to close friends or family members at any time. Whether you need to delegate some of the work, or simply need a shoulder to cry on, the planning stage is about so much more than two people. At the same time, if you're the one with the vision then ultimately the responsibility for making it come true falls to you.

In attempting to stage a ceremony and reception that literally nobody could anticipate, Liam found himself digging deep into his resolve. With a venue sorted, in the form of a windowless, concrete hangar on an abandoned military airfield, our groom confessed to feeling increasingly stressed about the miracle required to make it fit for purpose. 'It's unfortunate that once I've said I'm going to do something, I'll do it,' says Liam candidly. 'There was no changing my mind at that stage. I'm just not that sort of person. I just had to keep telling myself that Lynn's day depended on me getting it sorted, but it didn't make the obstacles any easier to overcome.'

Of all the challenges he faced, Liam considers his choice of wedding dress to be the toughest. 'As soon as I saw what he'd picked out,' says Lynn, 'I was devastated. It was filthy and riddled with holes. Part of me wondered whether it was a joke, and I just panicked. With one day to go, I seriously wondered what he was doing, and that's when the floodgates opened'. On receiving the news, Liam's upbeat nature took a nosedive. 'It felt like my whole world had come crashing down,' he says. 'If you don't get the dress right for a woman on her wedding day then you're a dead man. That's when all the doubts kicked in. I quickly sorted out a dress that she liked, but it was certainly my crisis moment. I thought if I can't even choose a decent dress then maybe I'd made a wrong decision about the whole event.'

Liam had just one solution to his loss of confidence. Quite simply, he shut himself off from any more sense of worry by just focusing on getting the job done. On the eve of his wedding, faced with single-handedly turning a disused military space into a venue fit for his bride, Liam experienced a long, dark night of the soul. 'I had so much stuff to do, but I was on my own. All I could do was roll up my sleeves and crack on. Basically, I just had to remind myself that if I didn't get it sorted then the guests would be turning up at a derelict site! In a way, it meant I didn't have time to fret. Staying busy is what got me through.'

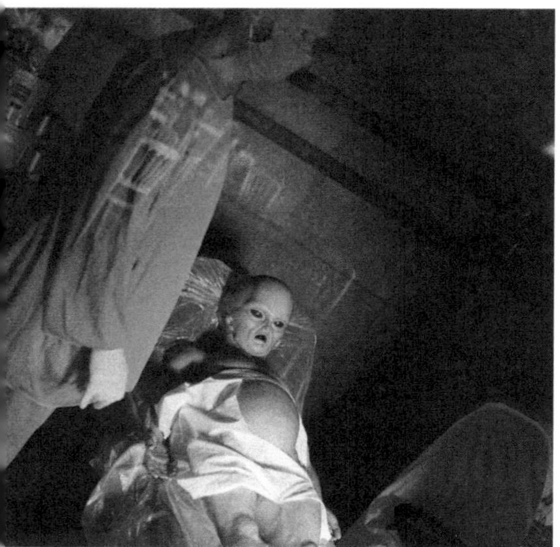

'You don't have to follow the rules to have a good time...'

Are Wobbles worth it?

So you've done your level best to lay on the wedding, dealt with all your doubts and worries, and now you're in the hands of fate. How does it feel, in that moment when you're preparing to reveal all? For Liam, it was a moment of high anxiety. 'I had gathered everyone inside the reception area, and closed the hangar doors. Lynn was on her way, and I just thought, "this is it." There was nothing more I could do but hope she didn't throw her flowers on the ground and walk away.'

Outside, having been escorted to the ceremony by military vehicle, Lynn admits to putting on a brave face. 'It was far from what I expected, and I didn't know what would happen next. Then these big metal doors opened, and it was the most amazing moment. As soon as I saw Liam, who looked like a broken man, I just thought "What have you been through to make this happen?" It was very emotional. I just wanted to hug him!' As

for Liam, setting eyes on his bride put everything in perspective. 'Nothing else mattered,' he says. 'Lynn was back in my arms, and everything from the preparations to all the worry just faded away.'

For Liam and Lynn, a madcap vision paid off on the day. Looking back, do the couple have advice for anyone else facing doubts about what kind of wedding to stage? 'Liam put his heart and soul into our day,' says Lynn. 'That told me just how much he loved me, though if I'm honest I'd suggest leaving all the planning to the bride!' As for Liam, he remains a firm supporter of the unconventional wedding. 'You don't have to follow the rules to have a good time,' he says. 'Coming up with an off-the-wall event might take all the planning and stress to another level, but as my stepson said on the day, it brought people closer together and with a lot of love.'

Highlights from the Show... The Night(mare) Before

Catherine and Richard – Home alone

It's the eve of her wedding, and the stress of not knowing how things are shaping up is threatening to get the better of bride, Catherine. All she wants, one simple thing, is the chance to spend the night in her own home in preparation for her big day. That's where she wants to get ready. Is that really too much to ask? Evicted for the last three weeks, so Richard can do all the planning, Catherine sits tensely on the sofa as the telephone call is made on her behalf. Richard's response? 'Impossible.' Which is the magic word, it seems, for a meltdown.

Jonny and Ayca – The hangover

'Oh...my...God!' This is Ayca's stunned response as she cracks open the door to her flat and surveys the aftermath of her groom's stag night. Frankly, it looks more like the place has been ransacked and vandalised than the venue for Jonny's goodbye celebration to life as a single man. 'They're meant to be organising a wedding,' she says, picking her way over discarded bottles, cigarette butts and clothing. 'Surely they haven't got time to have this much fun?' Then Ayca braves a look in on her bedroom, now trashed beyond recognition, and that's when her composure crumples. 'I want him to feel really bad for this,' she fumes.

Wesley and Rena – Car trouble

Adopting a fast-and-furious approach to his wedding, Wesley invites a bunch of flashy car enthusiasts to parade their vehicles on his big day. Then comes the last-minute news that a motor show is taking place at the same time. As a result, all the drivers have decided to pull out. Well aware that a car-themed wedding without any cars is just, well, a wedding, Wesley puts his foot down to make sure it's still a perfect day for his bride. OK, so the three performance cars that show up isn't quite a convoy, but what matters most is the fact that Rena is overwhelmed by the effort he's put into every other detail.

Linda and James – Kiss and make-up

Asking any groom to take charge of his bride's make-up for her big day is a tall order. No matter how much effort you put into it, chances are her tears are going to cause that mascara to run at some stage. Poor James puts in a huge effort to make Linda feel special, but falls short of expectation. 'It isn't me, and I won't be going out like this,' she says, before sobbing her heart out. Manfully, James rises to the challenge to ensure his bride looks radiant on the big day.

Dan and Mark – On notice

Dan is checking out his town hall venue of choice for his upcoming civil ceremony to Mark. It's shaping up to be just perfect, but for one minor detail. Legally, in order for the event to go ahead, Dan must give notice of their impending marriage. 'What's giving notice?' he asks sweetly, just moments before the penny drops. On learning that he must give notice 16 days before the ceremony, our groom does some panicky mental maths. On figuring out that he has just 24 hours or the whole thing is off, he resorts to understatement to hide the sheer terror in his voice. 'That's quite serious, isn't it?'

John & Jackie

What Were You Thinking?

As that well-known philosopher (and Facebook creator) Mark Zuckerberg once said: 'The biggest risk is not taking any risk...' But do you really want to take them at your wedding? If you stick to the norm there's always the danger that your wedding will end up being like everyone else's, but just how far are you willing to go to be different?

Whether it's dressing up as Disney characters or serving your guests sushi, you can make your special day as individual as you are. And if you do choose to do something daring and different, you can guarantee people will talk about it for years to come.

Jackie and John — The high flyers

Jackie and John's fate was sealed from the moment John spotted his future bride across the room at Kirkintilloch Miners' Club on the outskirts of Glasgow. Local lad John was a regular, but it was city girl Jackie's first visit to the down-to-earth haunt, and it's safe to say she wasn't wildly enamoured with either John or the venue.

She initially rebuffed his offer of a drink, but by the end of the night he'd won her over and the pair swapped numbers. 'We started dating at the end of 2005 and we did talk about getting married but as we couldn't afford it we didn't see any point in getting engaged,' explains Jackie. 'When I applied for *Don't Tell The Bride* I didn't think we had a chance. When we found out we'd been accepted John proposed almost immediately and we married just five weeks later.'

The couple definitely didn't have what you'd call a conventional wedding. In fact Jackie, who works as a project worker for children's charity Barnardo's, got the surprise of her life when carer John arranged for her to skydive into the wedding. 'The skydive was a

priority because I knew Jackie had always wanted to do one,' says John. 'I had a kind of blind confidence about it beforehand, but actually on the day I had a bit of a wobble. I was confident that she would do it but I wasn't sure how well it would go down. I was really hoping she'd love it.'

And she did. Sort of. 'Looking back on it now it was absolutely fantastic, but actually on the day I was horrified,' says Jackie. 'I'd had my hair and make-up done, and I was being driven to what I thought was the wedding venue. So when we pulled into an airfield I didn't know what to think. I thought maybe I was being flown somewhere and when I saw the "skydiving" sign all I could think was "this can't be happening". I know John says it's something I'd always wanted to do but it really wasn't. I'd made a flippant comment five years before that it might be fun but we'd never talked about it again. Initially, I wasn't sure if I was going to do it. But because I didn't have that much time to think about it, in the end I decided to go for it. I certainly won't do it again though!'

Christmas comes early

'If in doubt, ask your intended's friends and family for pointers, and don't be afraid to go for the obvious or just have a small nod to something you're passionate about.'

An element of surprise always makes a wedding more exciting, but will your other half really appreciate you hiring a burlesque dancer for the evening entertainment? You may love Take That but will your partner want to sing along raucously to a tribute act? In short, it's best to stick to things you know will go down well, and not just things you enjoy. If in doubt, ask your intended's friends and family for pointers, and don't be afraid to go for the obvious or just have a small nod to something you're passionate about. For instance, if you both love *The Tudors*, you could have a medieval feast rather than getting the entire wedding party to dress up in breeches and codpieces.

John always knew he wanted to do something unexpected for Jackie, so, even though the wedding took place in May, he used the fact that she's a massive Christmas fan to his advantage. 'Her love of Christmas made things dead simple because it meant I had something to focus on. May is a great time to get hold of anything Christmas-related because there isn't much call for it so it's really cheap. I decorated the reception venue with anything festive I could get my hands on, and we all sat down to a Christmas dinner. Jackie absolutely loved it, and so did the guests.'

Miner 'mare

'I was still kidding myself even as we were driving to the reception from the ceremony. When we first arrived I was so angry. I actually couldn't believe it...'

As much as risks can be amazing, if you're even slightly worried something may not go down well, steer clear. Sadly, no one told John that. In a classic case of 'what were you thinking?,' he made the decision to have the wedding reception at the place where he and Jackie first met – the Miners' Club. A resolute John explains why. 'I was always dead set on having some part of the wedding in the Miners'. It felt like things went full circle because that's where our relationship started. She was pretty let down when we first got there because it does look terrible from the outside. But when she walked in and saw how it had been transformed she forgave me. We worked really hard to make it look completely different.'

Jackie says she was initially dumbfounded when they pulled up outside the Miners'. 'People had joked to me that I was going to get married in the Miners' but I'd laughed it off. I thought there was no way John would do that to me. In my head it was almost too obvious. I was still kidding myself even as we were driving to the reception from the ceremony. When we first arrived I was so angry. I actually couldn't believe it. But when I walked inside and saw the hall I was thrilled. It took John and his mates four days to decorate the place and it looked incredible. I love the fact it was a bit ridiculous.'

John nose best?

'Forget cupcake towers or traditional tiers; he decided to have one of the most important components of the day modelled on Jackie's nose...'

Being quirky is one thing, offending people is another. What's funny to you may not be funny to other people, so avoid anything that could rub people up the wrong way. And remember your audience. For instance, while it may seem hilarious to name all of your tables after swear words to amuse your mates, bear in mind that your older relatives may not find it quite as humorous. In short, think things through properly before you dive in.

Thankfully one of John's other gambles did pay off. Forget cupcake towers or traditional tiers; he decided to have one of the most important components of the day modelled on Jackie's nose. 'She's always said that she wants a nose job so I thought it would be funny to have a cake in the shape of it. It could have gone horribly wrong but everything I did, I did for Jackie, with good intentions. I can imagine some women wouldn't have laughed if their partner had done that, but I knew Jackie would see the humour in it. The whole day was based around both of our personalities and to be fair we find most things funny.'

Take a vow

'It's up to you how much detail you want to add in, and whether you want to include all of the wording or just a general guide and information about hymns and prayers.'

Just because you incorporate some offbeat things into your big day, it doesn't mean the entire thing has to be one crazy rollercoaster ride. It's nice to keep some more traditional elements to your day so you strike a nice balance. And the vows are the perfect place to do that.

If you choose to have a religious ceremony, generally you're expected to have the traditional order of service. But you will have a chance to tailor it more to you by adding readings and music that mean something to you both. If you're having a civil ceremony you also have the opportunity to write your own vows.

While it's not a requirement, it's always a good idea to give an order of service to your guests so they know what to expect. The last thing you want is one of your bridesmaids popping off to the toilet at a crucial moment. It's up to you how much detail you want to add in, and whether you want to include all of the wording or just a general guide and information about hymns and prayers.

If you're confused about any aspect of the order of service you can always take advice from whoever is carrying out the ceremony. And if you do decide to make any changes, it's best to run those past them too before you make any firm decisions.

If you're having a non-religious ceremony or you just want to keep things more laid-back, you could choose to have a wedding programme, which is also referred to as an Order of the Day. This can cover both the ceremony and the reception. If the reception is at a different location it can also include travel advice, well as any info about the evening entertainment.

Even though the rest of their wedding was pretty unusual, John and Jackie wanted their actual ceremony itself to be fairly sedate. And, ironically, it ended up being John's favourite part of the day. 'The high point for me was the service because it was so lovely, and also seeing Jackie for the first time. I was totally blown away. I think we were both so happy with how it went. We had a humanist service, which is about your story and your relationship rather than god and religion. There was some real humour in it and some of our friends' speeches, and it was exactly as I'd pictured it.'

Go for it!

'Things don't always run one hundred percent smoothly, but sometimes that's a part of the fun…'

The one thing you want to be able to do is look back at your wedding day with a massive smile on your face. Things don't always run one hundred percent smoothly, but sometimes that's part of the fun. In Jackie's case, she could easily have flipped out over some of John's more 'daring' choices, but instead she embraced it as much as possible, and her memories are all the better for it. 'People say I stayed really calm throughout everything and I think a lot of that was because I'd seen so many episodes of *Don't Tell The Bride* so I knew what to expect. You can't do a show like that and think that everything is going to run smoothly. If you're the kind of person who panics, don't do it to yourself. I kept thinking to myself "what is the worst possible thing that could happen", and luckily it wasn't having my reception in the Miners', even though it wouldn't have been my first choice. People still come up and talk to us about our wedding now. We went clubbing after the reception and I was still in my wedding dress. It may not have been your standard wedding, there were some bits that were a bit crazy, but John put so much thought into it all that it made up for everything else.'

The happy couple, who now have a son Dexter, two, and another baby on the way, would advise anyone who is planning to think outside the box when it comes to their nuptials to go for it. As John says: 'I think you should take risks at your wedding and bring out your personality. I don't think enough people do that. People almost forget other people's wedding days because it feels like the same thing over and over again, and nothing funny or interesting happens. I've never been to another wedding like ours. I had indigestion for about six months after the wedding from the stress of it all but it was so worth it. It had been such a build-up so as much as I was sad when it all came to an end, it was a real relief. Having said that, I would definitely do it all again!'

Steve & Kayleigh

Lights, Camera, Action!

Your wedding photos will sit proudly on your mantelpiece forever as a reminder of your wonderful day, so you want to ensure they're everything you hoped for. That means choosing the right photographer – and planning ahead.

Steve and Kayleigh — What a ride!

When Steve and Kayleigh first started dating, things quite literally got off to a flying start. 'We met in a nightclub in Kingston and went on a few dates,' begins Kayleigh. 'He took me to the pub for our first date and he was painfully shy and I thought he was lovely. On the following dates, he took me to the cinema and to Thorpe Park, which is where he got the idea for our wedding. He says it was where he fell in love with me because I let my guard down for once. I'm scared of rides so he got to see the real me I guess. We were together for about two years before we got engaged.'

IT consultant Steve ended up proposing twice. The second attempt was a whole lot more romantic than the first, as well as being successful. 'The first proposal was awful, bless him. I badgered the life out of him until he put a ring on it and he ended up asking me while we were sitting in our front room. I'd been out with the girls for my birthday and he wasn't expecting me to come home as late or as half-cut as I was, but he asked me anyway. He used the same ring he'd bought me for my birthday so I wasn't very impressed, but he's made up for it since. The second proposal was seven months later at Christmas. He put together a little quiz and every time I got answer right I got to take down a piece of paper he'd stuck to our living room wall. When I eventually took them all down it said "will you marry me?" underneath. When I turned around he was down on one knee with a ring. So yes, I got two proposals. I'm so greedy it's ridiculous!'

Park life

'In an ideal world he would have got me a chav-tastic blinged-up tracksuit like the one Britney Spears had for her wedding so I could have worn that.'

Kayleigh – who is a full-time mum to Gray, seven, Dexter, five, Blake, two, and baby Octavia – applied for *Don't Tell The Bride* and even filled in the form on Steve's behalf. 'I was watching the show with a friend and like most people I was always saying I could do a much better job. Steve and I really wanted to get married but we already had two sons so saving was out of the question, so I thought why not?'

'It was stressful organising everything but it went really quickly,' says Steve. 'I didn't stop from the minute we knew we'd got a place on the show but it was a good laugh getting the lads together and trying to plan what to do. I had a few ideas and then Thorpe Park popped into my head and it seemed like a great idea. As Kayleigh said, it was where I fell in love with her so it seemed fitting. I thought the day went really well overall.'

Well, apart from Kayleigh freaking out when she arrived at Thorpe Park, of course… 'The thought behind it was sweet as a button but it was pretty horrific,' she says. 'I like to think I masked my horror quite well but I really didn't. I couldn't believe he'd chosen a theme park as our wedding location. I was supposed to go on one of the rides but it was impossible because my dress had a massive hoop in it so I couldn't close the safety bar. Steve's excuse is that because he doesn't wear dresses he didn't realise. In an ideal world he would have got me a chav-tastic blinged-up tracksuit like the one Britney Spears had for her wedding so I could have worn that. If I hadn't been in my dress, I would have gone on it 100 percent. I did actually go on later once I'd changed, so I'm not a total wimp. Aside from Thorpe Park, I had a brilliant time. Seeing Steve after three weeks of being apart was amazing. That was the best bit for me. Being back together as a family felt great and I have some amazing memories.'

Picture perfect?

'Photographers generally cost around 10 percent of the overall wedding budget so pick wisely!'

It goes without saying that finding a good wedding photographer is essential if you want your wedding pictures to have the 'wow' factor. So what's the best way to go about finding one? Recommendations are always great as you're getting first-hand information, and obviously the internet is a great resource. Also, consider going along to a wedding fair where loads of snappers will have their portfolios on display for you to look through. Don't feel pressured into making a decision on the day though. Take home brochures and have a proper look through before you make your choice.

Photographers generally cost around 10 percent of the overall wedding budget so pick wisely! Also, bear in mind that some photographers specialise in certain areas so there are many things to consider:

- **Do you want a modern, traditional or fly-on-the-wall feel?**
- **Do you want photos taken inside, outside or a mixture of both?**
- **Do you want your pictures to be colour, black and white, or both?**
- **Is it more important for the photos to illustrate your love story or give a broader picture of the day?**
- **Do you want a videographer as well? And if so, will you be able to negotiate a better price if you hire both together?**

Here's a list of good things to ask potential photographers:

- **How far in advance do they need to be booked?**
- **How much of a deposit do they want?**
- **How many weddings have they photographed?**
- **Do they have references?**
- **How happy are they to take instruction?**
- **How long do they expect to spend at the wedding?**
- **Is yours the only event they're working at that day?**
- **Are they happy to look round the venue beforehand?**
- **Are they better shooting in black and white or colour?**
- **What are their total costs, including an assistant and printing?**
- **How much will they charge for extra prints?**
- **Would they allow you to have a CD of all the images so you can print them yourself?**
- **Who retains the copyright for the photos?**
- **If they do, will they ask your permission before using your images anywhere else?**

Kayleigh and Steve were lucky enough to have two photographer friends who helped them out on the day. But because of time limits, they didn't get all the shots they hoped for. 'Things were a bit of a rush on the actual day so we didn't get nearly as many photos taken as we'd like to have done,' says Kayleigh. 'We didn't have a chance to get groups of family and friends together, which is a shame. We have got some beautiful pictures that are very natural, but not many posed ones. We didn't have any pictures taken at Thorpe Park either. After we got married I changed so I could go on a ride, and the only one we've got is the snap they take of everyone as you're zooming round. It's a brilliant wedding photo though. It's hilarious.'

Thankfully, the family all still had their outfits so, much like the proposal, Kayleigh and Steve simply decided to do everything twice! 'In the end we actually went back to Oatlands Park Hotel in Weybridge, where the wedding took place, and had our photos redone,' explains Kayleigh. 'We still had the suits and my dress, so we all smartened up again and got a whole load of new pictures. Sadly, the best man and bridesmaids weren't there so we haven't got any formal ones with them in, which I was gutted about, but we made the best of it.'

Needless to say, the couple didn't need a videographer as they had their own film crew in the shape of the BBC capturing every moment. As Steve says: 'We didn't have a videographer because everything was being filmed so that became our wedding video. We went to a wedding where they had a videographer and they asked people to record nice messages for the couple at the end of the night, but everyone was really drunk so a lot of them ended up being pretty lewd. If you're going to have a videographer it's probably a better idea if they film early on!'

Snap happy

'It's good to have a solid plan of action and know exactly what you want from a photographer...'

To ensure your photos are exactly what you want it's a good idea to spend time with your photographer before the event and, if possible, take them along to do a tour of the venue so you can show them exactly what you want and they can pinpoint good picture opportunities you may not have thought about. They're there to capture the spirit of the day, so the more information they have upfront, the better.

As Kayleigh says: 'I think it's really important to have a good relationship with the photographer so you can ask them to get photos of what you want. There's no point in being nicey-nicey and not having your say. Everyone thinks a wedding day lasts so long but it goes in the blink of an eye. It feels like everything's been speeded up so you need to be fairly strict about it.'

Steve agrees that it's good to have a solid plan of action and know exactly what you want from a photographer. 'I would recommend that people have set times for the photos so you know what's being shot and when. I didn't so that's why we missed out on so many pictures on the day. Also make a list of the photos you want so you have a plan and you can get it done as quickly as possible instead of standing around thinking what you want to do next. Obviously, if other photo opportunities come about then great, but definitely have some kind of strategy.'

Your photos are potentially going to be passed down through generations and there's a temptation to try and document every second of the day. But how much is too much? Do you really want your photographer running down the hall after you while you pop to the ladies? Is it appropriate for them to snap you as you're having a cheeky shot at the bar with your mates?

It's also important to think about how much time you want to set aside for pictures because you don't want to spend hours outside posing while your friends are inside having fun.

'I was bridesmaid to a friend of mine, and Steve even had to go and check into the room without me because we had such a strict photography schedule. It did feel like a military operation, but they got what they wanted,' says Kayleigh.

Insta-glam

'Photo booths always go down well with guests and people love the cheesy dressing-up element too. They're always a fun reminder of a good night...'

These days, thanks to camera phones, everyone is a potential photographer. So if you like the idea of your pictures having more of a reportage feel, ask your mates to snap away till their heart's content. Even though they missed out on having a full set of official photos on the day, they still had masses of unofficial ones to choose from thanks to theirmates' pics.

As Kayleigh says: 'There are loads of photos on Facebook that we've printed off so that's been great, and we also took some ourselves. I love an Instagram filter because it makes everything look better so I made good use of that! Our friends probably captured things an official photographer wouldn't, so we ended up with a huge choice.'

Camera phones aren't the only way to get additional shots. You can leave disposable cameras on the tables for guests to use, and photo booths are becoming increasingly popular at weddings. Not only are they tons of fun, they also provide a way for guests to have their own memento of the day to take home with them.

Kayleigh is definitely a fan. 'Photos booths always go down well with guests and people love the cheesy dressing-up element too. They're always a fun reminder of a good night. At the end of the day, who doesn't like sticking on a wig when you've had a few drinks?'

Highlights from the Show... Lights, Camera, Action!

Sian and Anna – Strike a pose

Tomboy Sian freely confesses to knowing next-to-nothing about how to string together a girly wedding for fiancée, Anna. Choosing the right bridal dress proved a struggle, one that even turned to disappointment, and Anna is beginning to wonder whether the love of her life is too far out of her depth. Then the morning of the wedding dawns. After three weeks of what Sian describes as 'worry, stress and tears,' she comes up trumps with a charming photographer that brings out her bride in nothing but smiles and sets her up for the day.

Nathan and Nikki – Photos in the frame

Sipping tea with her family before the big day, Nikki outlines how every wedding should pan out. When it comes to the timetables, she tells her mum, there is a way of doing things, and photography is compulsory. 'Two o'clock – "I do," she begins, before taking her through the rest of the day. 'Chat, chat, chat, meal, meal, meal. Milling. Drink, drink, drink.' And then... 'Photos! Snap, snap, snap. Back in, back in. Sit, sit, sit. Eat, eat, eat. Speech, speech, speech. Dance till one o'clock in the morning. Done.' If only Nathan had got the memo.

Joe and Emily – The busman's holiday

A wedding photographer by profession, bride Emily has high hopes when it comes to capturing her special day. For groom Joe and what's left of his budget, however, this is just one more aspect of the planning process that's causing him to stress out. Fortunately, friend Dan is on-hand with a smart solution. 'Why don't we tell all the guests to bring cameras or just have disposable cameras dotted around the place? Then we'll put the photos together and make an album to send to everyone. It would work out a lot cheaper. Fifty quid max!' Joe weighs up the cost-saving against his future wife's expectations, and beams.

Paul and Emily – No pictures, please

Spend-aholic Paul has blown the budget for his wedding to Emily, and forgotten to cost in a photographer. It leaves him no option but to put in a pleading call to the hotel in a bid to cancel the rooms he's booked for friends and family. Fortunately for his guests in need of accommodation, but not for Paul, it's too late to back out. Enter mum, and a generous loan, which enables our groom to book a last-minute snapper that arguably saves the day.

Mitch and Laura – That special moment

Bride Laura is at home and ready to roll. She's resplendent in her bridal gown, and hiding her disappointment that Mitch hasn't sorted a photographer for those 'getting ready shots'. As it turns out, her future husband has ensured that the pre-wedding preparations are recorded for prosperity. Down at the beach for a final surf as a single man, he's brought along a good friend and pro-photographer to capture the moment. Whoops.

Andy & Serena

Speeches

Speeches are one of the most important and nerve-wracking parts of any wedding. From projector-led spectaculars to brief but heartfelt readings, there's no right and wrong. Whether you're speaking for yourself or someone else is doing it on your behalf, you want it to be meaningful and make an impact.

Andy and Serena – The perfectly mismatched pair

Serena and Andy first met as teenagers, but they weren't ready to settle down together until some years later. 'We were 14 and 15 when we first met through friends,' begins Serena. 'We became girlfriend and boyfriend, but we later split up and then got back together in our early twenties. It wasn't long before we moved into our own place and got engaged. Andy proposed while we were on holiday in Spain and we were surrounded by family and friends. I wasn't expecting it at all but it was really romantic and I loved the ring he chose.'

The couple say it's insurance broker Serena who wears the trousers in the relationship. While Andy is laid-back, she describes herself as 'naggy and bossy' and even admits she bought their first flat in Bristol without consulting him. Despite all of that, she was strangely happy to hand over the responsibility of organising her big day to Andy. 'It was Andy's sister, Beverley, who suggested we enter for *Don't Tell The Bride* and I thought it would be a really interesting, fun thing to do. I was quite shocked when I found out that every single bit of the organising would be left to him, but at the same time I found it quite exciting.'

'Neither of us had spoken that much about what we wanted to do wedding-wise so I kind of had a free rein,' continues Andy. 'Serena isn't one of those women who has been planning her wedding since she was a little girl and tearing things out of magazines, so that made things a lot easier for me.

> **'I had never planned to speak myself because it's my worst nightmare standing up in front of people, but I did get on the microphone later in the night and thank everyone. I kept it very short but I wanted to show how grateful I was and I'm glad I did...'**

If she'd had really strong opinions on the day and wanted every little detail to be perfect, there's no way I would have done it.'

Bristolians Andy and Serena are now parents to five-year-old Lexi and two-year-old Jenson. Serena says that while she found it hard handing over control of the wedding to Andy, she has no regrets. 'It was really tough moving out of our flat and leaving our dog, and knowing I wouldn't see Andy for a month was so strange. But, in the end, the day was perfect and went really well. I couldn't have asked for anything else really. Everyone I wanted to be there was there and we all had such a good time. I'm glad I took the risk and let Andy do what he wanted. He did me proud and it's a day I will never, ever forget.'

Brotherly love

Salesman Andy had been a rock to Serena's family. Her half-brother, Dean, and half-sister, Chan, see him as an older brother, and he wanted the wedding to be a success for them as much as Serena. Serena's dad left before she was born and her mum later split up with her stepdad, leaving Serena without a father figure to walk her up the aisle. That duty fell to Dean, who also gave an emotional father-of-the-bride speech. 'He was brilliant. Everyone was so moved by what he said. I knew he was really nervous but he did an amazing job,' says Andy.

The sight of her brother speaking so emotionally proved too much for Serena, and she soon found herself wiping away tears. 'I cried the whole way through Dean's speech. He was only 16 and he'd never done anything like that before. And then on top of everything else it was being filmed which made him even more nervous. When he said it was the proudest day of his life that was it, I just went. I had never planned to speak myself because it's my worst nightmare standing up in front of people, but I did get on the microphone later in the night and thank everyone. I kept it very short but I wanted to show how grateful I was and I'm glad I did.'

Despite Andy's worries that his best man Alan may overstep the mark with his speech, thankfully he managed to keep things light-hearted and, well, fairly tasteful. 'Alan did a great job. You never know what he's going to say so it was a risk letting him do a speech. His opening joke was about being an alcoholic so I think that kind of set the tone. Serena and I just looked at each other and shook our heads. He made a joke about fancying my sister and that was the only thing that really made me cringe. I was worried he'd take things too far and say something dodgy in front of my gran but thankfully he was well behaved. He was surprisingly nervous and I didn't expect that from him because he's pretty outgoing. I know he spent a lot of time on the speech and he did a great job. It was a good mixture of funny and meaningful, which is what I think a speech should be. He'd been by my side throughout everything and the speech topped everything off brilliantly. He was a legend.'

I'm still standing

'If you're following formal etiquette, the father of the bride usually speaks first. It's his job to thank the guests for coming, welcome the groom to the family, say something lovely about his newly married daughter and then toast the happy couple...'

Speeches usually follow the wedding breakfast, but there are no hard-and-fast rules about when you have to have them. It's becoming increasingly popular for people to start them as soon as everyone sits down to eat, which means that those who are making speeches can relax and enjoy their meal (it also ensures they're not half-cut by the time it's their turn to speak!).

If you're following formal etiquette, the father of the bride usually speaks first. It's his job to thank the guests for coming, welcome the groom to the family, say something lovely about his newly married daughter and then toast the happy couple.

The groom comes next and he usually kicks off by thanking the father of the bride. He then says a few words about his beautiful new wife, hands out thank-you gifts to bridesmaids (and the best men if they're lucky enough) and toasts the bridesmaids.

If she chooses to speak the bride usually goes next. She often thanks the bridesmaids and anyone else who has helped out. She may say a few words about her groom and choose to read a poem or do a short reading.

The best man is last to go. It's his job to tell the story of how the bride and groom got together, and then share a series of amusing and often shameful anecdotes about the groom. At the end of his speech he proposes the final toast and everyone basically uses it as an excuse to drink the rest of their champagne.

If you want to skip the speeches and keep things short and sweet it's perfectly acceptable to just do a series of brief toasts. In fact, sometimes people find this preferable. While speeches can be enjoyable, there's nothing worse than a dedication that lasts for hours when everyone is desperate to go to the toilet or kick off the disco.

Lost for words

'My advice to anyone would be not to overthink it…'

Not sure how to give a great speech? Here are some tips:

- **Know your audience. That hilarious story about how you and the groom once got arrested on a night out? Not so funny if his mum didn't know anything about it. That brilliant tale about the strip club his new wife didn't know he'd been to on his stag do? It's best left out. Speeches are all the better for having some humour in them but you don't want to potentially break up a marriage before it's even begun.**
- **Avoid the internet. It's incredibly tempting to go online and copy massive chunks of standard speeches to incorporate into your own, but people will spot plagiarism a mile off. As much as anything else, it won't come across as genuine. If you need help or pointers ask a friend or family member, not Google.**

- Keep it short. This cannot be said often enough!
- Make sure everyone in the room can hear you. If you're speaking to a large group of people it's advisable to get a microphone so that those people who have been hidden away at the back can enjoy your words too.
- Rehearse your speech in front of an attentive friend, family member or partner before you unleash it on a room full of people. That way you test out your jokes, see if the heartfelt stories are moving enough and still have time to tweak it if need be.
- Thank the right people. Be certain you know whom to thank before you stand up. It's not uncommon for people to extend their gratitude to hairdressers, make-up artists, florists, and caterers – the works. If you're doing a best man or best woman speech ask the bride and groom beforehand for a list of acknowledgements. You don't want to leave anyone out.
- Remember it's not about you (unless you're the bride and groom, in which case it kinda is). It's easy to go off on a tangent and talk about yourself in relation to the happy couple. But, as harsh as it sounds, unless you're one of the newlyweds, guests aren't going to be that interested.
- Make sure people have a drink before you ask them to raise a toast. It's good to give them a warning along the lines of 'ladies and gentleman, I shall shortly be asking you to charge your glasses so please ensure you have something nice to drink'.

Andy admits that his speech was one of the trickier parts of his day. The fact that he didn't have anything planned out didn't help matters. 'I had no idea I was supposed to speak so I didn't have anything prepared. I'd organised everything else but a speech hadn't even entered my mind. My plan was to say something simple like "thank you for coming. Have a good time", but then I got told I had to thank everyone individually. It went okay in the end but had I known in advance what was expected of me I would have made much more of an effort.'

However, the fact it was so impromptu did have some benefits. 'Because it was sprung on me at the last minute I didn't have time to get nervous or think about it too much. So maybe it actually all worked out the right way?' says Andy. 'I knew that both mine and Serena's family would want me to keep things quite light and it did end up being like that. Looking back, the only thing I regret is not complimenting Serena enough. She looked so incredible but I was trying too hard not to leave anyone out of the thank yous that I forgot to tell her that.'

Now he's had some first-hand experience, Andy has some helpful hints for anyone who's going to be stepping into his groom shoes. 'Speeches are getting harder and harder because weddings are getting so

big and people take a lot more time over them these days. My advice to anyone would be not to overthink it. Do some research and know what you want to say but don't write a firm script because then there won't be any kind of natural flow to it and it may seem stilted. It's a good idea to write down some key words to use as a prompt, but then I would say to improvise as much as possible.'

Serena is in total agreement, and also suggests keeping the speeches brief and to the point. 'We went to one wedding where three people spoke for about 40 minutes each and it was too much. They all pulled out a wedge of paper and you knew what was coming. In the end the kids started getting really restless so I had to take them outside. It was a bit of a relief, to be honest. Some people did a sweepstake on how long they thought the speeches would take because they were going on for so long. It was ridiculous. I feel like ours were just the right length and everyone said what they wanted to, which was the important thing.'

Highlights from the Show... Speeches

Andrew and Amanda – The best man says goodbye

Throughout the run-up to the wedding, best man Neil has been a constant presence at Andrew's side. Some might see this as more of a hindrance than a help, as Neil tries in vain to bring out Andrew's laddish side. With our groom focused on marrying martial arts expert, Amanda, it's down to Neil to come to terms with the fact that Andrew's bachelor days are over and wish them both every success. Which he does with a heartfelt speech and then a bid to join in with their first dance. 'You're my best man,' says Andrew, smiling through gritted teeth, 'and that's as close as you get, you know?'

Mike and Katie – Lost for words

'I didn't realise I'd be saying anything,' says the groom from the top table at his own wedding reception. 'So, I've not prepared anything at all.' To be fair, having thrown himself into the planning process over three intense weeks, Mike can be forgiven for this one oversight. At the same time, he recovers well with a combination of charm, sincere thanks to his friends for supporting him and family for attending, plus the ability to simply wing it through to the end. With a supportive crowd, gathered at Blackpool Winter Gardens to celebrate the happy couple's new life together, Mike can be congratulated on a job well done.

Ian and Jay – What happens in Thailand...

It's traditional for the groom to hold his breath when the best man rises to give his speech. Ian expects a few jokes at his expense, but not the breaking of a stag night secret he's yet to share with Jay. As the guests gasp at the revelation, the groom sees no choice but to roll up his sleeves and explain himself. 'Alright, so, absolutely plastered I managed to get *Don't Tell The Bride* in Thai tattooed on my arm,' he says sheepishly, prompting the woman in white at his side to rest her head in her hands.

Rodney and Paula – Absent friends

As well as bringing people together, weddings are often a time to remember those who can't be there to mark the happy occasion. As she prepares to marry the love of her life, Paula's late father is in her thoughts. Her loss leaves Rodney all the more determined to make the day special. Touchingly, his efforts are recognised in a moving speech from the bride's sister. 'My dad would've been so proud of you today,' she says, 'for doing what you've done for Paula... Thank you. You've made him happy.'

Jason and Cassy – Old Jokes

A long time before they tied the knot, Jason and Cassy attended the same primary school together. With their lives so entwined, it stands to reason that when the groom makes his speech it's going to come from the heart. Having staged Cassy's dream ceremony, and a reception enjoyed by friends and family, Jason kicks off by announcing that this isn't the first time he's risen from his seat that day with a piece of paper in hand. When you've just married your soulmate, old jokes are totally allowed.

Nathan & Nikki

The Music of Love

No wedding would be complete without a soundtrack. At best, it's the element of your day that can amplify the emotions and make the special moments truly memorable. From marking the bride's arrival at the ceremony to filling the dancefloor at the reception, and even seeing off the happy couple as they embark on their new lives together, this often-overlooked feature can actually help to define the day.

But when it comes to selecting the music, just how can you be sure that you're striking the right notes? With so many elements to consider, from the type of wedding you have in mind to your personal taste, there's always a risk that this aspect of your planning can turn to angst. The last thing you need is for your guests to giggle when the organist strikes up, or even make an exit because your DJ won't leave the microphone alone. Then there's the band you booked that fails to turn up, or decides to showcase new material, and the neighbours you forgot to notify, who insist on pulling the plug early. In short, without due care and attention music has the potential to make or break your day. On the upside, by making full use of your ears as much as your heart and mind, it's perfectly possible to ensure that the sounds at your wedding transform the day into a momentous and magical event.

Nathan and Nikki — Pomp and pageantry

Blind dates often bring together people from different walks of life, with interests and personalities that don't immediately seem like a match. Often, such dates don't go any further than an evening that both parties can chalk up as an interesting encounter. But when they do evolve into something more meaningful, it can lead to a unique bond that often proves unbreakable.

On paper, Nathan's interest in history, pomp and circumstance wouldn't appear to make him a natural fit for Essex-born hairdresser Nikki and her fun-loving personality. Against all odds, however, the pair enjoyed an intense

romance before Nathan acknowledged that he'd met his soulmate by popping the question. 'We are polar opposites,' he admits, 'but there was an instant connection between us from the first date.' Above all, Nathan was drawn to the fact that he and Nikki are just so different. 'I'd hate to marry someone like me,' he says. 'It would be awful. We'd only argue all the time.'

For a man who nominates Trooping the Colour as a favourite childhood show, and even describes himself as 'Prince William at rest', his engagement to Nikki was less than ceremonious. 'He'd planned to propose to me on New Year's Day but couldn't wait,' she jokes. 'At the time I was rolling up socks. The pair of us were in our pyjamas as well, but to be fair I did say yes!'

As the happy couple clearly show, opposites really can attract. But what happens when it comes to tailoring a wedding to suit both bride and groom? When your interests are so different, how can you be sure it'll be in tune with your individual hopes and dreams? 'I wanted something pink, feminine and girly,' says Nikki. 'I was worried he might do something pretentious, but I didn't think he'd want our guests going "this is awful!"'

Given sole responsibility, Nathan had every intention of giving his bride the perfect day. Even though his vision was far from Nikki's idea of a dream wedding, he felt sure that one element in particular would play a vital role in winning her over. 'I was seeing history, pomp, pageantry, oak panelling and portraits,' he says, 'but the music is just so important to get right in terms of mood and poignancy. On your wedding day, whatever you choose will turn out to be part of the soundtrack of your lives.'

The sound of your wedding

Before making any decisions about music, it's vital that you're clear what kind of wedding you have in mind. A religious service, for example, may come with certain traditions and expectations, while a civil ceremony could be so open to interpretation that it's hard to know where to start. Whatever you choose, always consult with the individual in charge of the service, such as the minister or registrar. Not only will they be able to provide guidance, and offer up ideas, they can serve as a sounding board for your suggestions based on wisdom and experience. Ultimately, you want to be confident in your selection, and not fretting on the day that you might've missed the mark.

Committed to a vision for their wedding day, and knowing just what style of music would underpin it, Nathan consulted a source that he could trust: his iPod. 'Every day I make a 50-minute drive to and from work, and this was the perfect opportunity for me to listen to loads of tracks. Even so, I knew what composer I wanted to feature right from the start. In my mind, Handel was perfect for just about every significant moment of the wedding'.

So what are the key times that you need to consider? Depending on the type of ceremony you choose, here's a general guide:

Prelude

We're talking about that period when your guests begin to gather. It's an exciting time, but often conducted in hushed and reverent tones. Generally, people take their places and chatter quietly in expectation, so it's down to you to underscore the moment in a way that doesn't overwhelm. It might be tempting to dazzle, but ultimately your congregation are focused on settling into their seats

Pre-processional

We're beginning to build up to the main event now. This is when key players such as the families of the bride and groom arrive, along with all the other special guests. In making your musical choice, the aim here is to suggest that the best is yet to come. So keep your cool, and be sure not to upstage the main event.

Processional

Here come the stars of the show – the wedding party! This includes the arrival of everyone from the bridesmaids to the flower girls, the best man and groom, and, last but not least, the bride accompanied by her father (or the individual chosen to give away her hand in marriage). Music-wise, think big. Whether we're talking traditional hymns or something contemporary and even unconventional, make sure your music selection also comes with a sense of respect for the occasion. This is a momentous event in your life, after all, and deserves to be marked appropriately.

Ceremony

Traditional weddings call for traditional music during the service. You may have more freedom to choose at a civil ceremony, such as a performance by a solo instrumentalist, but still it's important to reflect the gravity of the occasion. Also consider your music for the moment that the newlywed couple sign the registry. In a way it's a break for your congregation, so they might well have keener ears. The nature of the event will dictate what's fitting, as well as the duration, but opting for something low-key and contemplative should work well with the moment.

Recessional

You've done it! The knot has been tied and now the happy couple turn to beam at their guests as they exit the ceremony. Even if you've opted for a formal approach to your wedding, this is where the music should aim to be joyous and uplifting. Many couples also put careful consideration into the music that accompanies that slow shuffle of your guests as they leave their seats and turn their attention to the reception.

Keep music live (but not always)

'Opting for recordings to mark the service gave Nathan peace of mind. It also freed him up to focus on the main event, while allowing him to stage a live-music surprise to herald the couple's arrival at the reception: a trumpeters' fanfare!'

There's nothing like the sound of real instruments. Compared to a recording, most people would agree that it can't be beaten. A live ensemble, a solo musician or even a band could well bring out the very best from the musical element of your wedding, but there are considerations to be made. Cost is a central factor, of course, and compared to the price of a few CDs you could be looking at a significant portion of your budget. You also need to be sure that your chosen act can deliver the goods. This might mean checking them out in performance before you commit, or at the very least hearing a demo. The last thing you want to discover is that your musical attraction isn't quite as note-perfect as they promised, or comes with a list of demands that takes the shine off your enjoyment of the day.

For many couples, a mixture of live performance and recordings provides a balance that makes the music selection both manageable and rewarding. For Nathan, adopting this dual approach provided him with a level of control over the way their big day played out. Opting for recordings to mark the service gave him peace of mind. It also freed him up to focus on the main event, while allowing him to stage a live-music surprise to herald the couple's arrival at the reception: a trumpeters' fanfare. 'It was very grand,' reflects Nikki. 'It was also something only Nathan would think to do, and I knew how much thought he had put into it. I loved it!'

With the formalities over, Nathan was keen to make sure that the right music continued to capture the moment. 'For our first dance, I chose "Time After Time" by Cyndi Lauper,' he says. 'After all the bombast, the pomp and pageantry, it just felt completely natural to go for a simple, three-minute love song that means a lot to both of us.' As they took to the dance floor, Nathan's choice clearly connected with Nikki, who was transported back to the early days of their relationship. 'On our second date, he'd serenaded me with that song on his guitar,' she says. 'He's such a romantic deep down!'

Having struck the right chords throughout their day by choosing music that befitted each moment, appealed to him and tweaked Nikki's heartstrings, Nathan finished with a chance for their guests to slip on their dancing shoes. 'We had a cheesy disco,' he grins. 'It was a fun, family affair, and everyone just had a really good time.'

Music review

Looking back on their wedding, Nathan acknowledges just how much work had gone into it. Like any ceremonial event, the timing was key from start to finish, and this is where he has words of advice for couples considering how music fits in. 'On the day, you need to let someone manage it who isn't the bride or the groom. Everything from tapes to recitals need to be synchronised so it goes off at the right moment and at the correct volume. So, once you've made your music choices, and worked out the logistics, having somebody you trust take over just makes things so much more relaxed. As the bride and groom, you're the centre of attention. There can be so much going on that having the micromanagement of the music off your mind basically takes away all that pressure.'

With so many competing factors that feed into planning a wedding, it's easy to place music far down the list of things to sort out. From experience, both Nathan and Nikki believe it's something that deserves a great deal of attention, and pays off on many different levels. 'Sound is one of the five senses,' Nathan points out, while acknowledging that everyone has different music tastes. 'So whatever you choose, just make it heartfelt. Nothing else matters to be honest. I might have done loads of research into the music that went with the ceremony, and put in hours of listening to different versions, but at the end of the day the one choice that felt so important to us both was the track for our first dance. It really was as simple as that.'

Highlights from the Show... The Music of Love

Stuart and Vicki – Band on the run

Marrying a music lover should mean the sounds will be in good hands for your big day, right? Bride Vicki is left to wonder as Stuart sets out to string together a day to remember. Having proposed to Vicki at a Turin Brakes' gig, he even roped in the band to help mark the moment, he now sets his sights on actually booking them for the big day. Cue nearly three weeks of hovering over a phone, waiting for the band's management to call... and politely decline. The result? Vicki's dream of castles and cut-glass crystal is downgraded to a boozer and a busker, and turns out to be everything the couple could've wished for. 'It's just beautiful,' beams the bride. 'I'm on cloud nine!'

Cameron and Sarah-Jane – You can't sari love

Determined to honour his multicultural heritage, Cameron takes his new bride away from the reception for a moment so he can present her with a gift. 'It's a sari,' he says, fishing the garment from a carrier bag. 'That is so cool!' squeals Sarah-Jane, who promptly ditches her wedding dress to make a grand reappearance in honour of the wedding's Indian theme – just in time for the couple's first dance. It's enough to shift up a gear in the celebrations, and brings everyone out to join in.

Hywel and Beca – Wonder-wedding

In getting hitched to his beloved Beca, groom Hywel attempts to bring a flavour of the Glastonbury festival to Bridgend. With music forming the central pillar of their day, he ropes together his brother, best man and Beca's son to record a very special version of Oasis' 'Wonderwall' in his back garden. Production values might be left wanting in places, but it makes up for that in sheer passion and sincerity. For Beca, on seeing the video for the first time, it reinforces every reason why she said yes to her man in the first place.

Wayne and Leanne – Sing if you're wedding

'I'm dreading the day,' confesses Wayne, but his love for Leanne is not in question. It's what he's expected to perform that's brought him out in a cold sweat. 'Why, why, WHY?' he wails. 'Why do I have to sing to her?' Because, Wayne, you're honouring a promise you made to your fiancée a long time ago, and it wouldn't be good to break that on your wedding day. The groom recognises this for himself, and briefs the band he's booked to prepare for a special guest appearance. Come the big day, with the speeches over and the dancefloor filling, it's time for Wayne to face the music. With the microphone in hand and a rictus grin across his face, he draws breath… and it turns out he really can hit the right notes! Warning: may not work for every groom.

Afterword

I always cry at the ceremony, because as part of the *Don't Tell The Bride* team I know how much the couples have been through to get there.

In the three weeks before the wedding, I've witnessed those moments when the groom feels he can't do it, when he's had to pull himself together and push on because everything depends on him.

So, when he finally sees his bride, after weeks apart, I'm rooting for her to recognise his efforts. Like the viewers, I want her to see that even if he got some things wrong, ultimately he's done it for love.

Sarah May
Executive Producer, *Don't Tell The Bride*

List of Photographs

All images courtesy of Alamy and Shutterstock, except the following:

Andrew Hazard Photography: pp. 180, 183, 184, 185, 186 and 187
Darren and Bronte: pp. 28 and 32
Barry Phillips Photography: pp. 154, 159, 160 and 162
Sally Wilkinson Photography: pp. 108, 111, 112, 114, 115 (t), 117, 119
David Lane: pp. 92, 95, 96, 99, 100, 101, 102, 103, and 104–105
Fern Buckley-Jones: p. 136
Ryan Walker: pp. 66, 69, 70–71, 72, 75, and 76
Rian Palfrey: p. 44
Steve and Kayleigh: pp. 219 and 225